The BLOB Book

Cassia Dee

This Book Belongs To:

Introduction

As a disabled & chronically ill woman, traditional art advice has never been possible for me to follow. I could never keep up or be what I was told an artist needed to be, and because of this I thought I could never be a "real" artist.

All of that changed when I started a 222-day challenge where I focused on healing my creativity by embracing it exactly as it was. This meant that no creative act was too insignificant or too small, and it meant that everything I did mattered and was enough. I called this perspective Gentle Creativity.

Gentle creativity helped me see that I am an artist, limitations and all. It gave me permission to take a million baby steps and to believe in myself in a way I never had before, and because of this the book before you was born.

I designed The Blob Book to be a quick, creative escape for the average, busy person, as well as a more accessible art book for disabled or chronically ill people. I know that for many people, myself included, the time, strength or health required to complete art prompts is not always attainable, and I wanted a book that was created with that in mind.

Blob art has become one of my favorite art practices, but more than that it has become a safe place for my creativity to thrive. My hope for this book is that it can become the same for you.

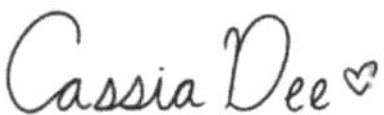

Instructions

1. Flip through the pages, choose a blob, and make it something all your own
2. If you're feeling stuck, rotate the book and look at the pages from another angle
3. Don't stress or worry about making something "good"
4. Embrace the mess, the silly, and the ugly
5. Relax and have fun!

Category ideas to get you started:

-Doodles
-Characters
-Shapes
-Faces
-Patterns
-Foods
-Landscapes

-Fantasy
-Abstract
-Plants
-Monsters
-Animals
-Cartoons
-Architecture

I would love to see your doodles, messes, creations, and masterpieces! Share them on social media using #blobbook.

Tips For the Paper In This Book

1. Place a piece of thicker paper (I cut mine to the size of the book) behind the page you are using to help prevent your art supply from bleeding onto other pages and ruining them.

2. Test your materials on the test page at the back of the book to avoid unexpected results. Some of my favorite art supplies to use on this paper are listed on the following page, but feel free to experiment with what you have.

3. Avoid watercolor paints.

4. Be careful with water-based markers. I love using cheap markers, but the trick is to not be heavy-handed when coloring and to allow each layer to fully dry. Also, keep in mind that water-based mediums can warp and buckle the pages.

5. All markers will probably bleed through the paper, but that won't be a problem if you apply my first tip. ☺

My Recommended Art Supplies

- **Ballpoint pens.** If I could only use one medium in this book, it would be a simple black pen. Writing pens don't require any setup or color picking, and you can use them anywhere! You can also get fancy and use fineliner/inking pens if you want, but never underestimate how fun blob art can be even with the cheapest pen you have.

- **Crayons.** Crayons are great for encouraging an extra playful approach and are a good choice when trying to avoid perfectionism. They are also a great option for kids.

- **Markers & colored fineliners.** I find the darker colors in my sets the most useful, but be careful about bleed-through and tearing the paper (see my marker tips on previous page).

- **Acrylic paint pens.** Definitely one of the most fun options!

- **Colored pencils.** I use colored pencils the least often in this book, simply because they tend to be the most time consuming. However, they are a lot of fun and are the most versatile option if you have time for them. Just be aware that different brands work better than others on this paper.

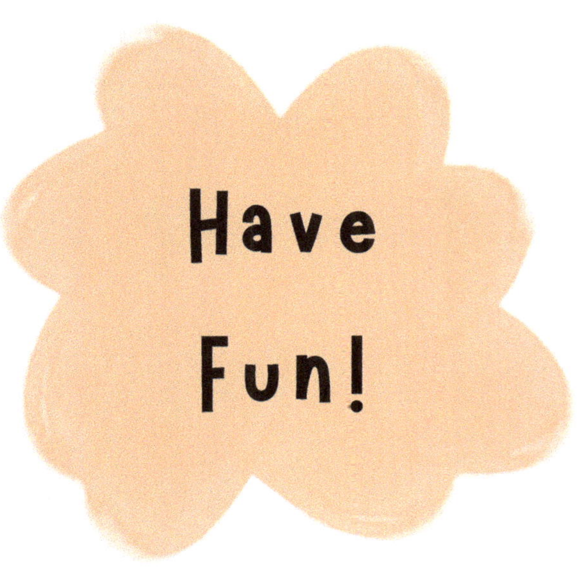

Have
Fun!

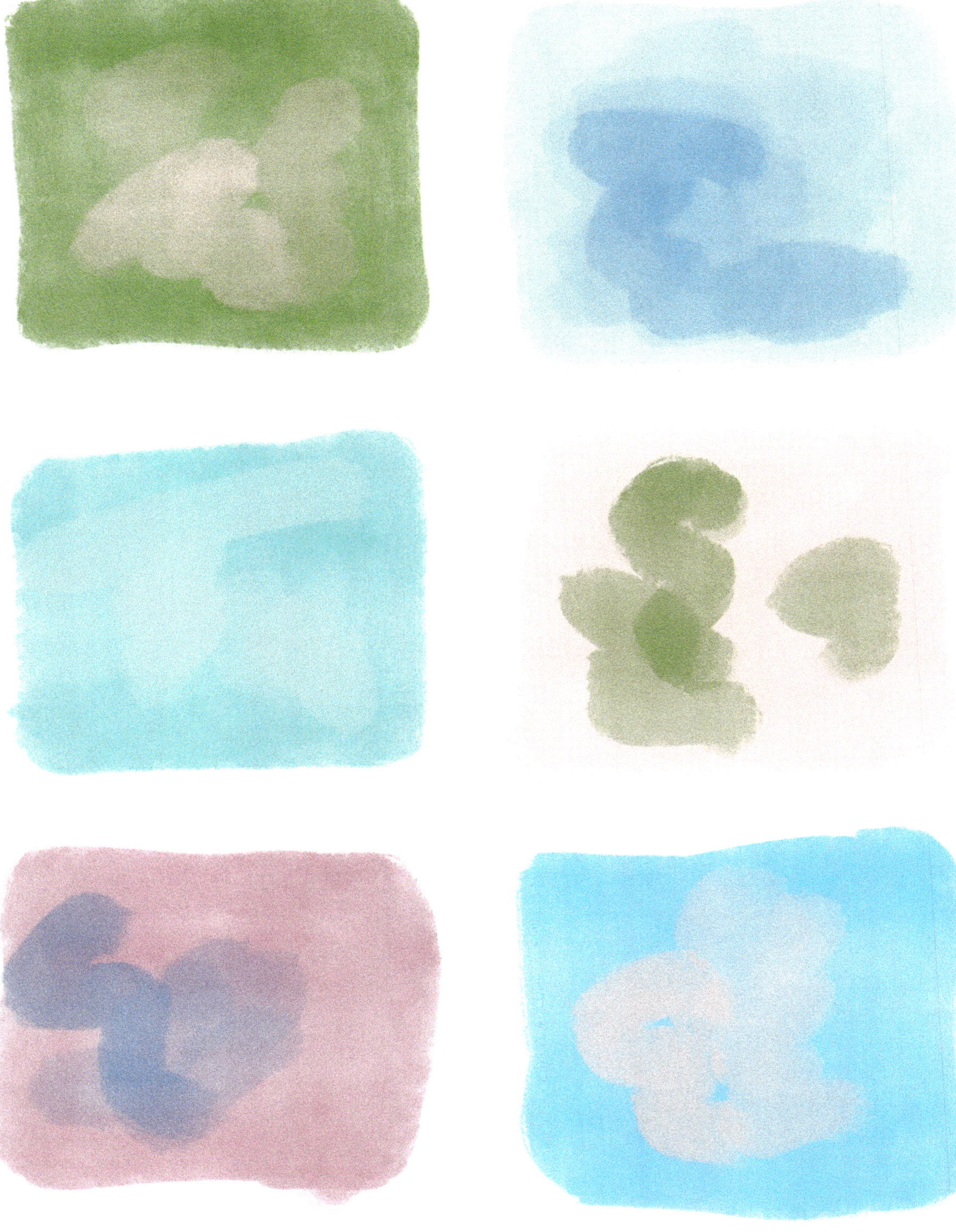

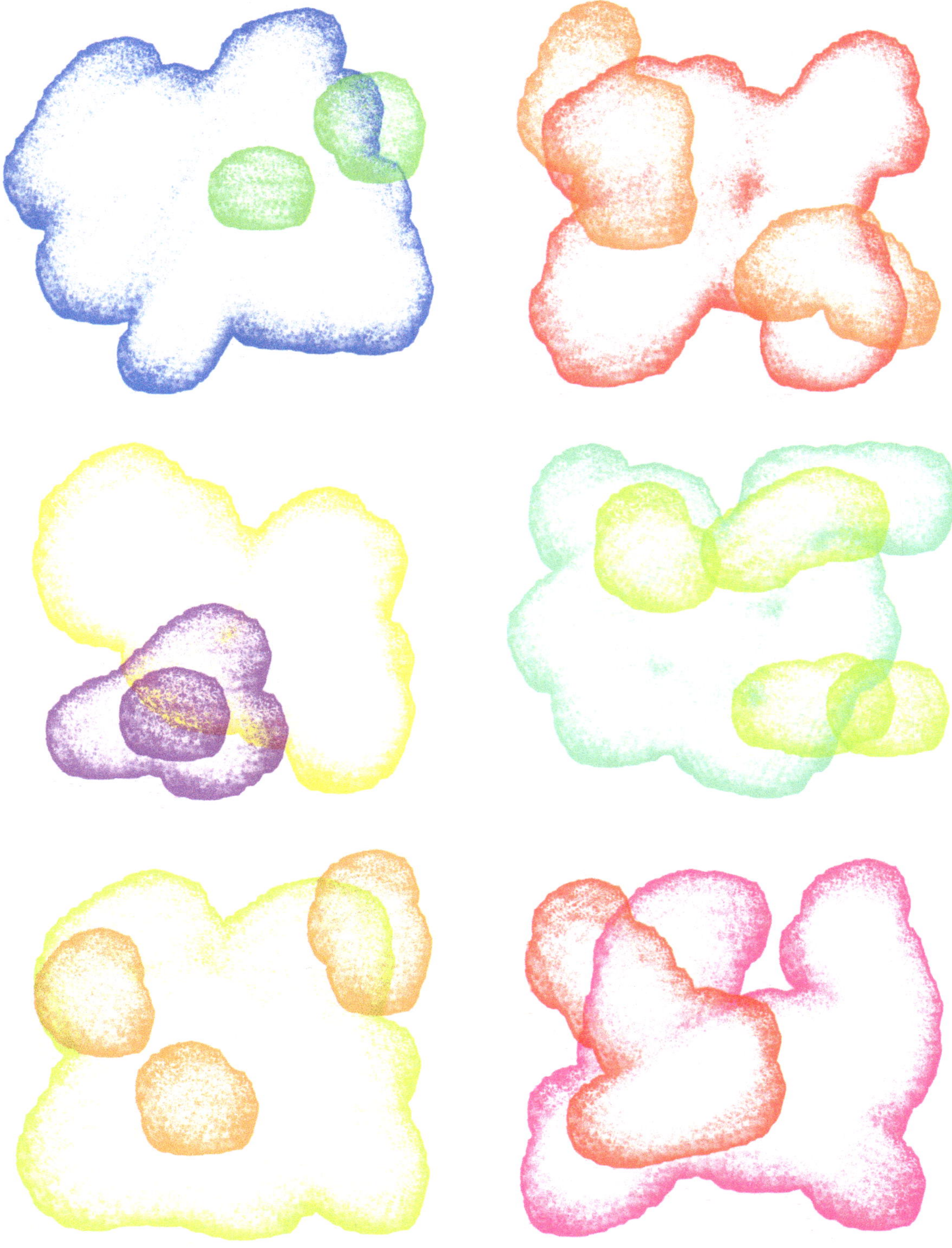

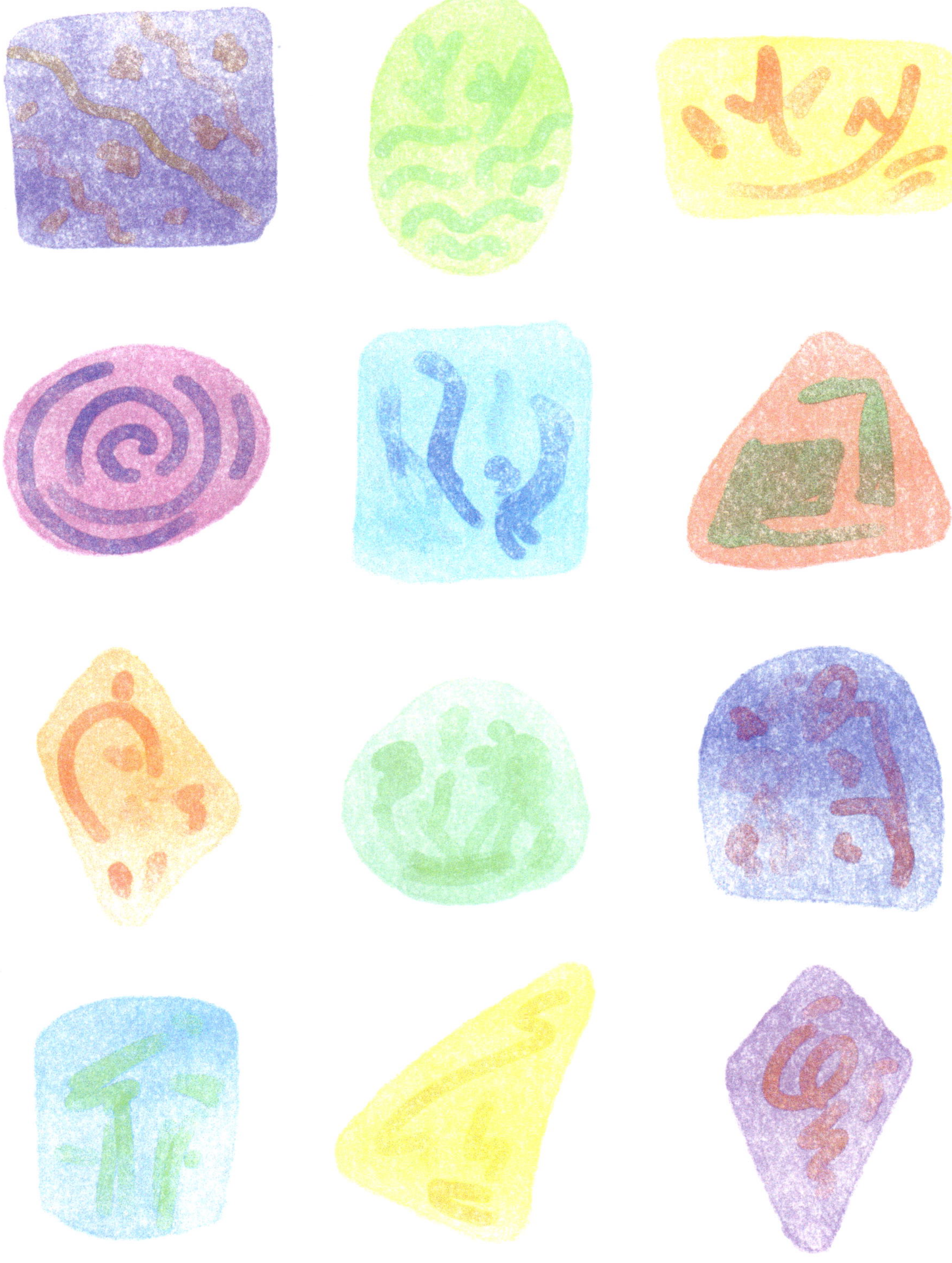

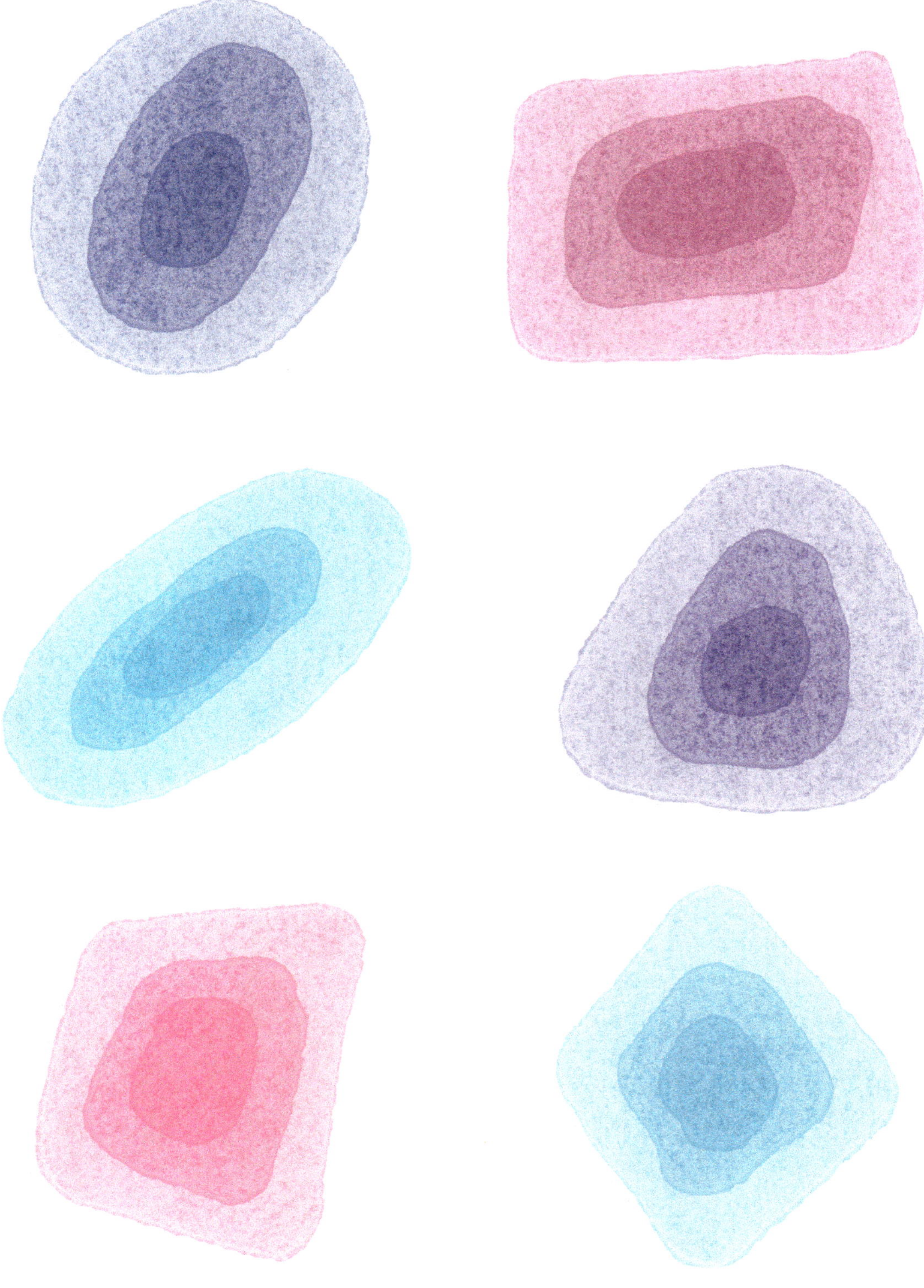

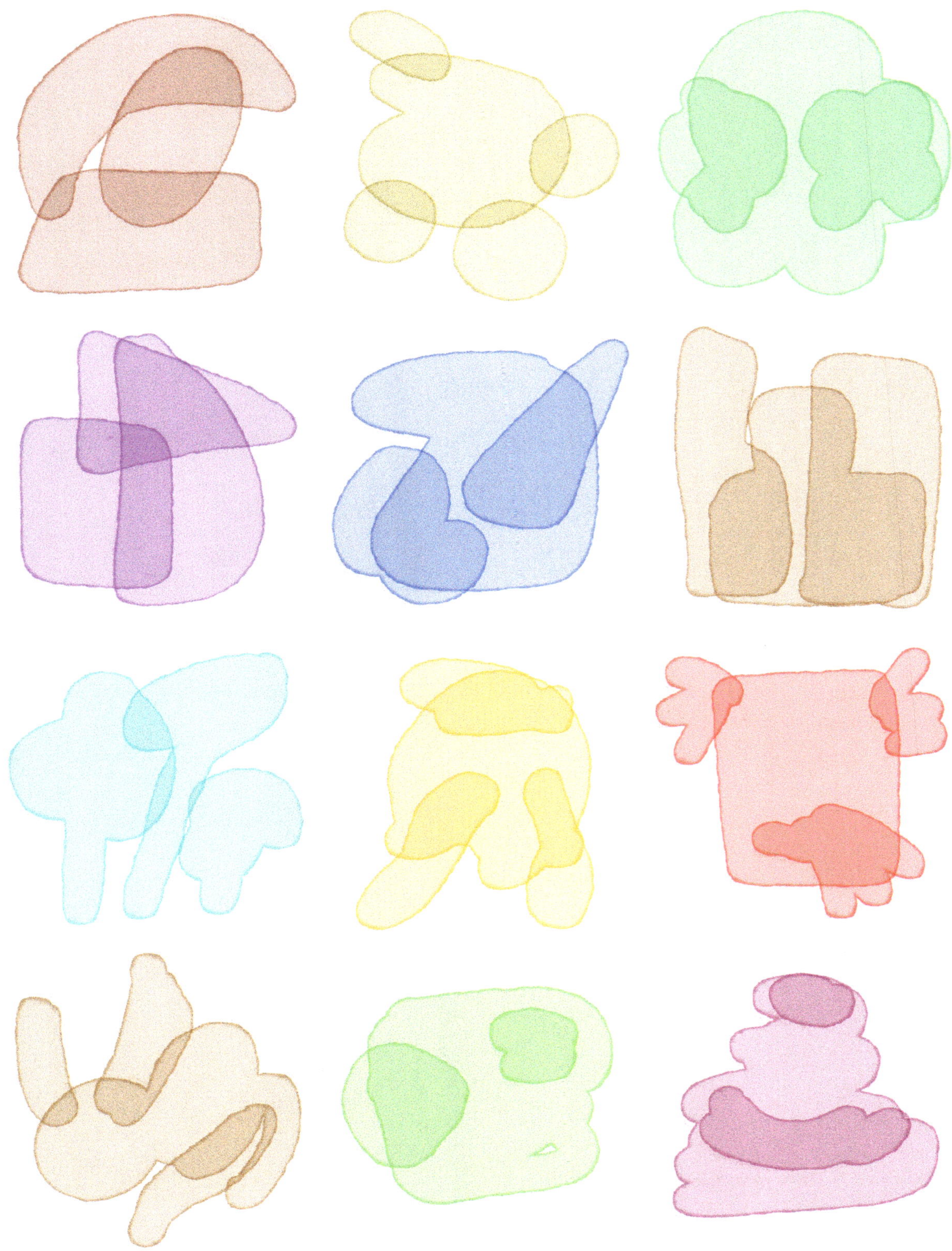

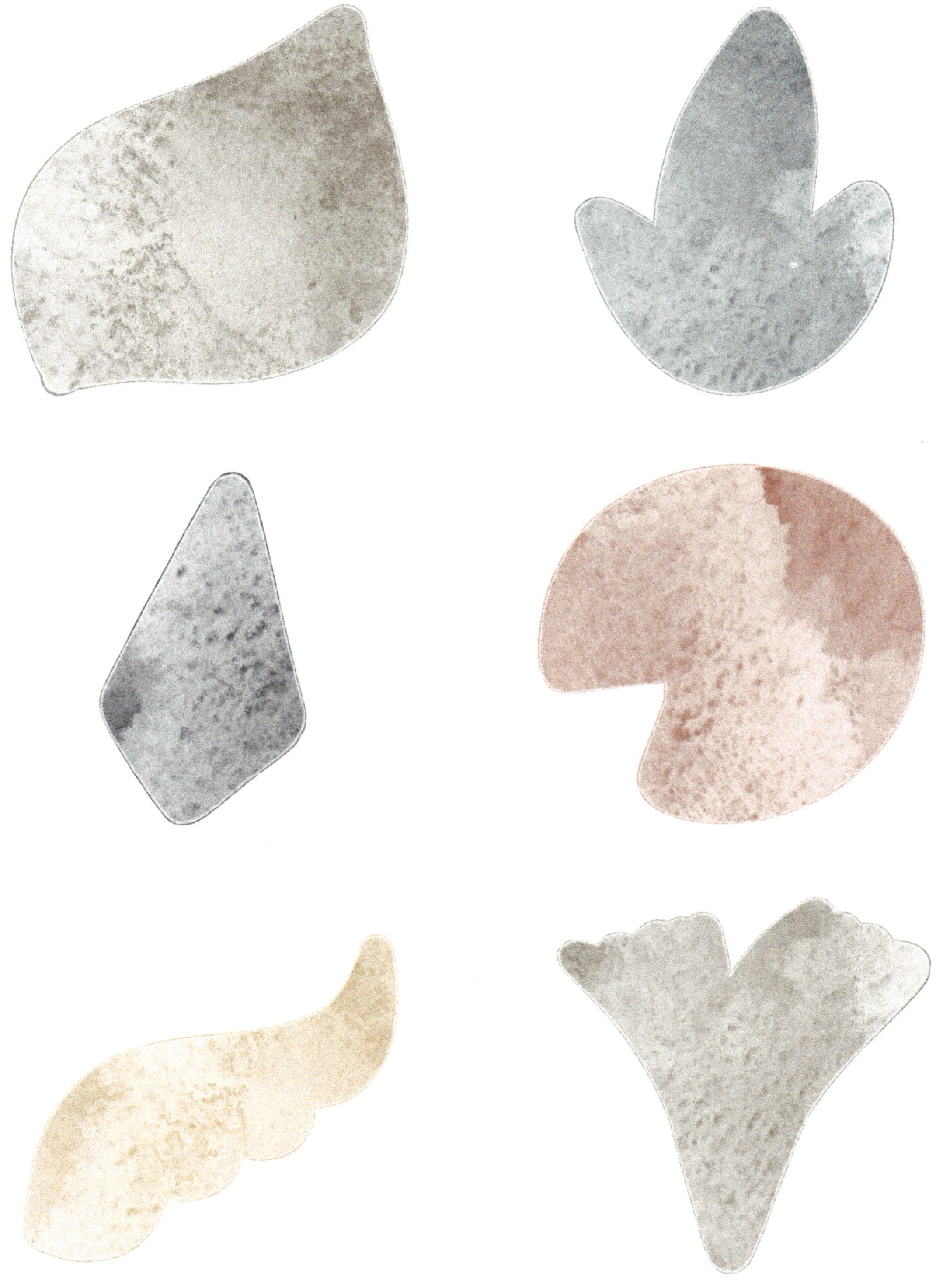

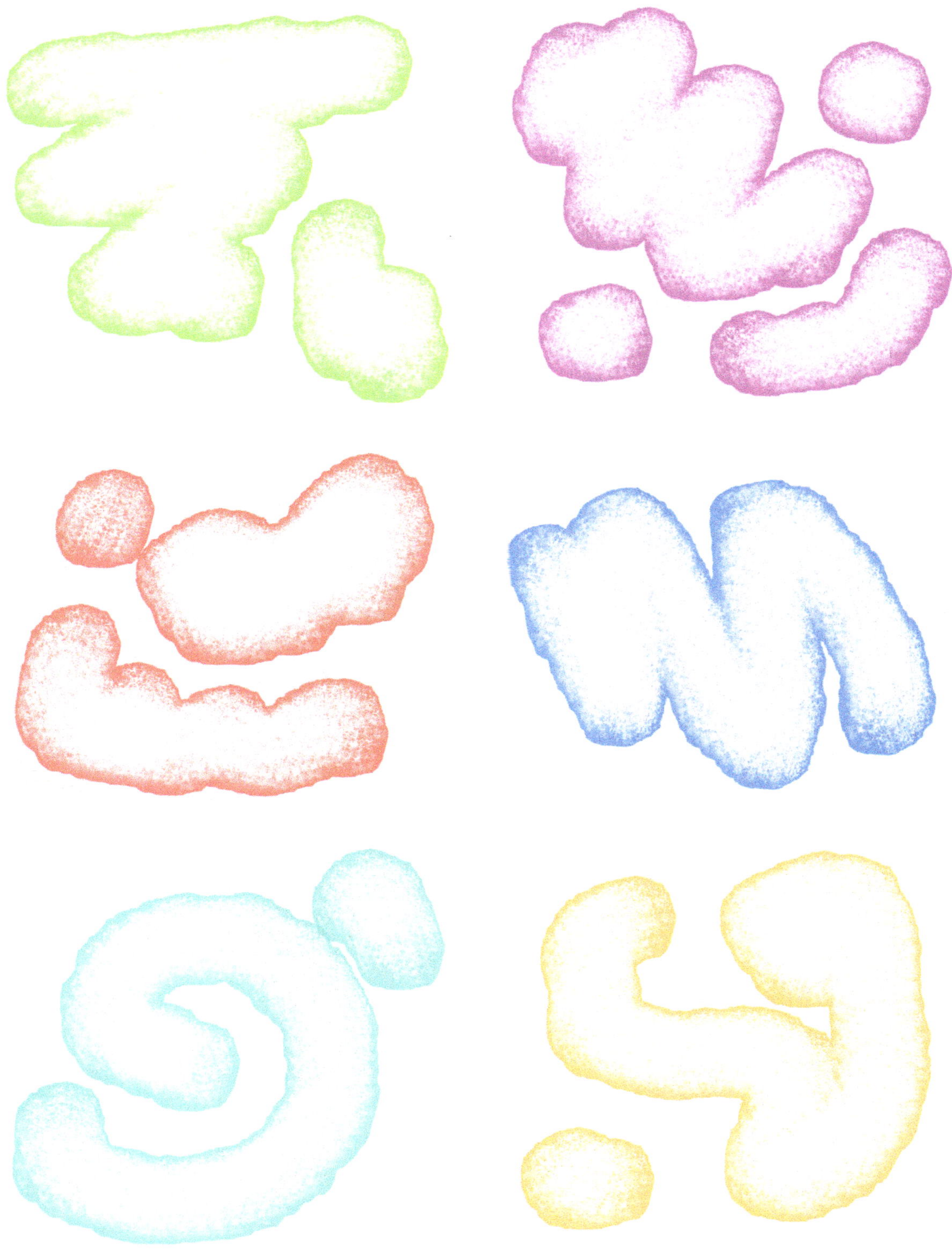

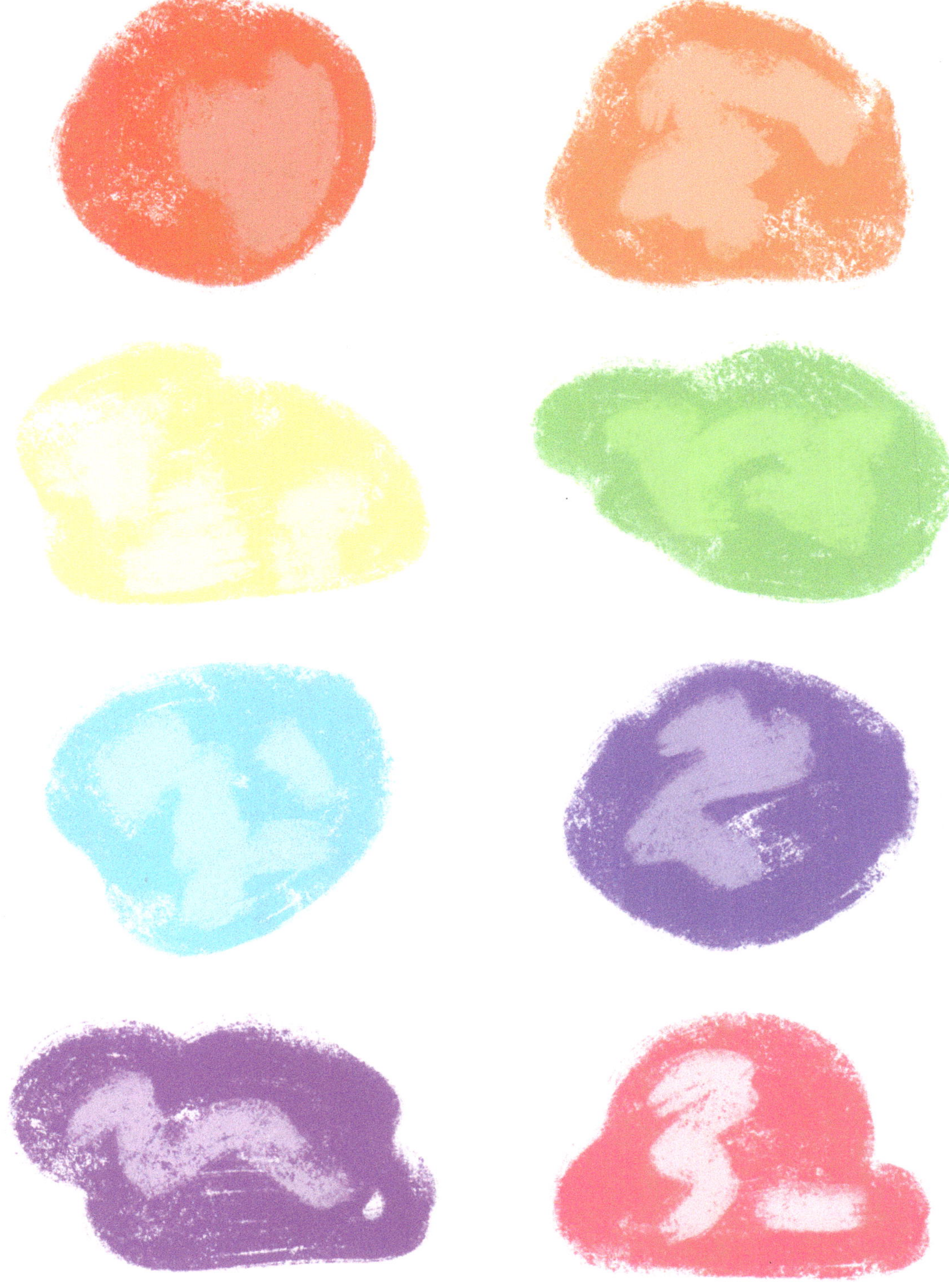

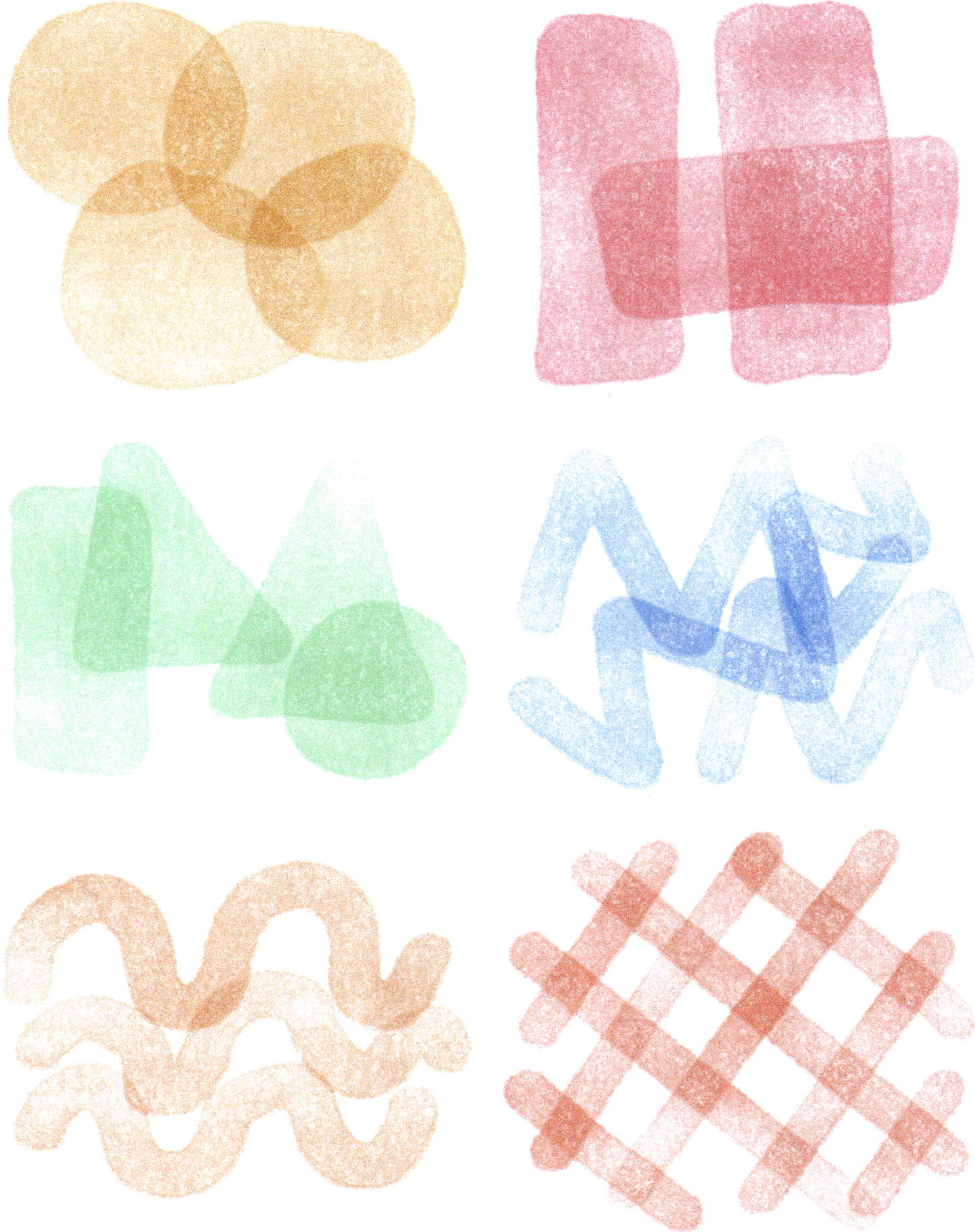

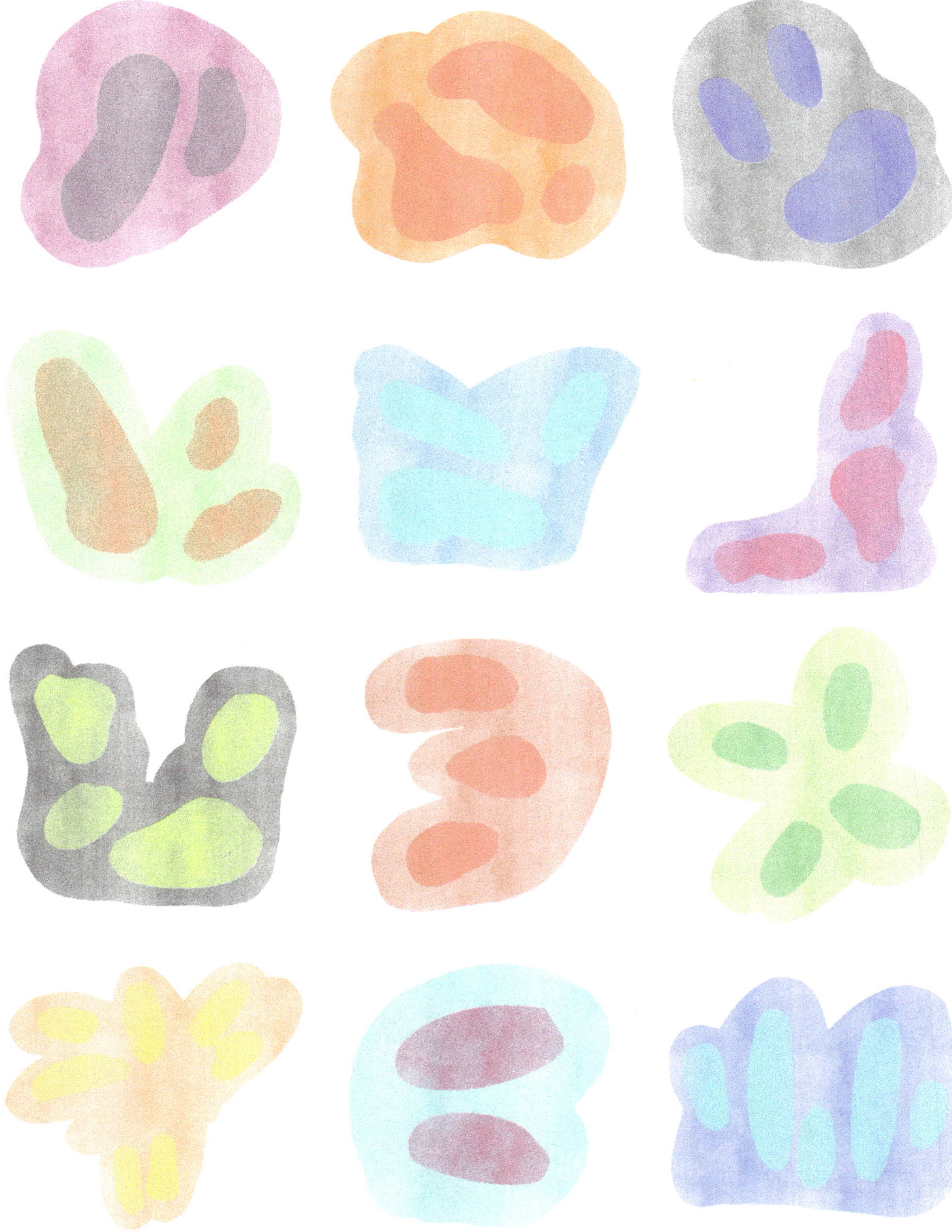

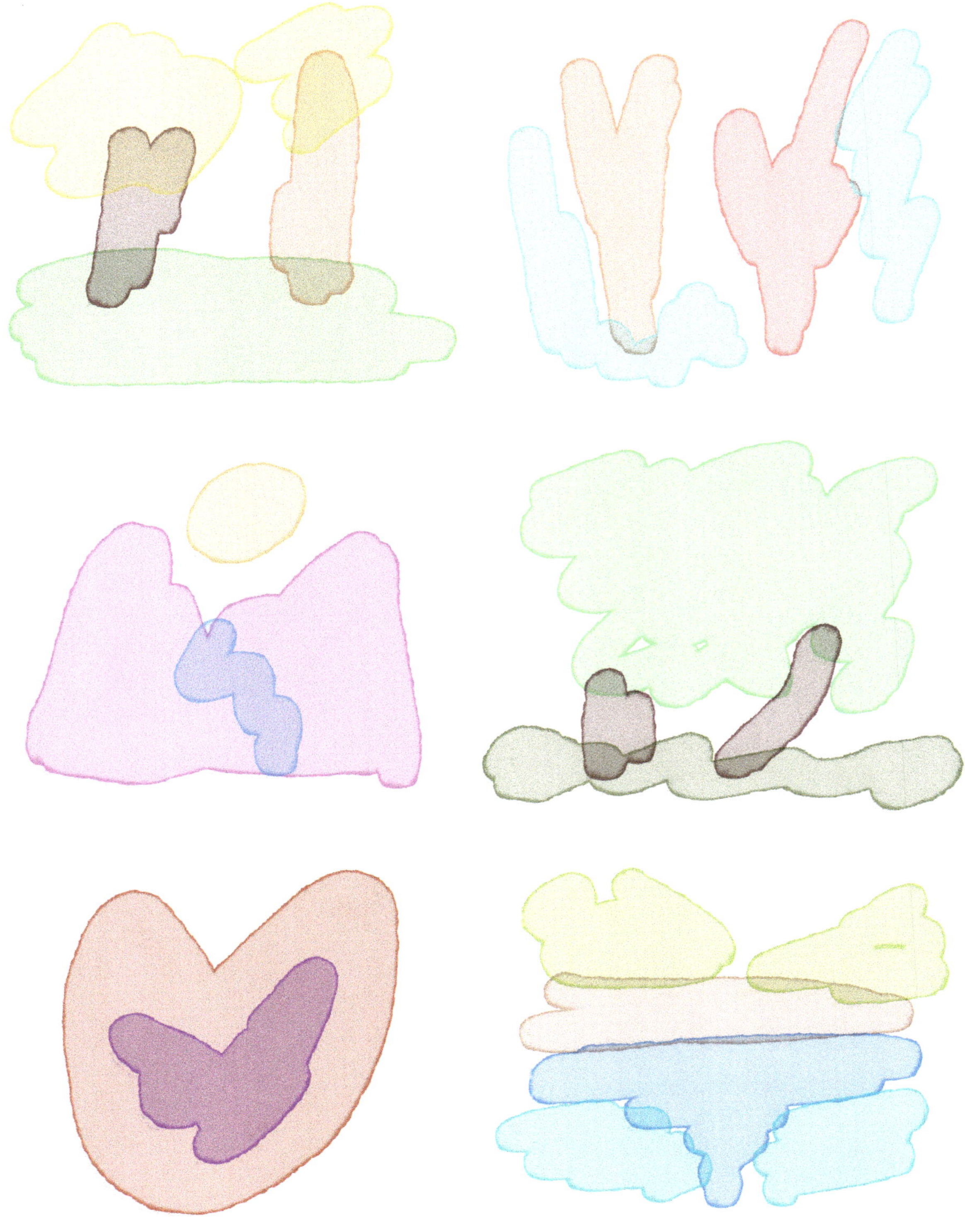

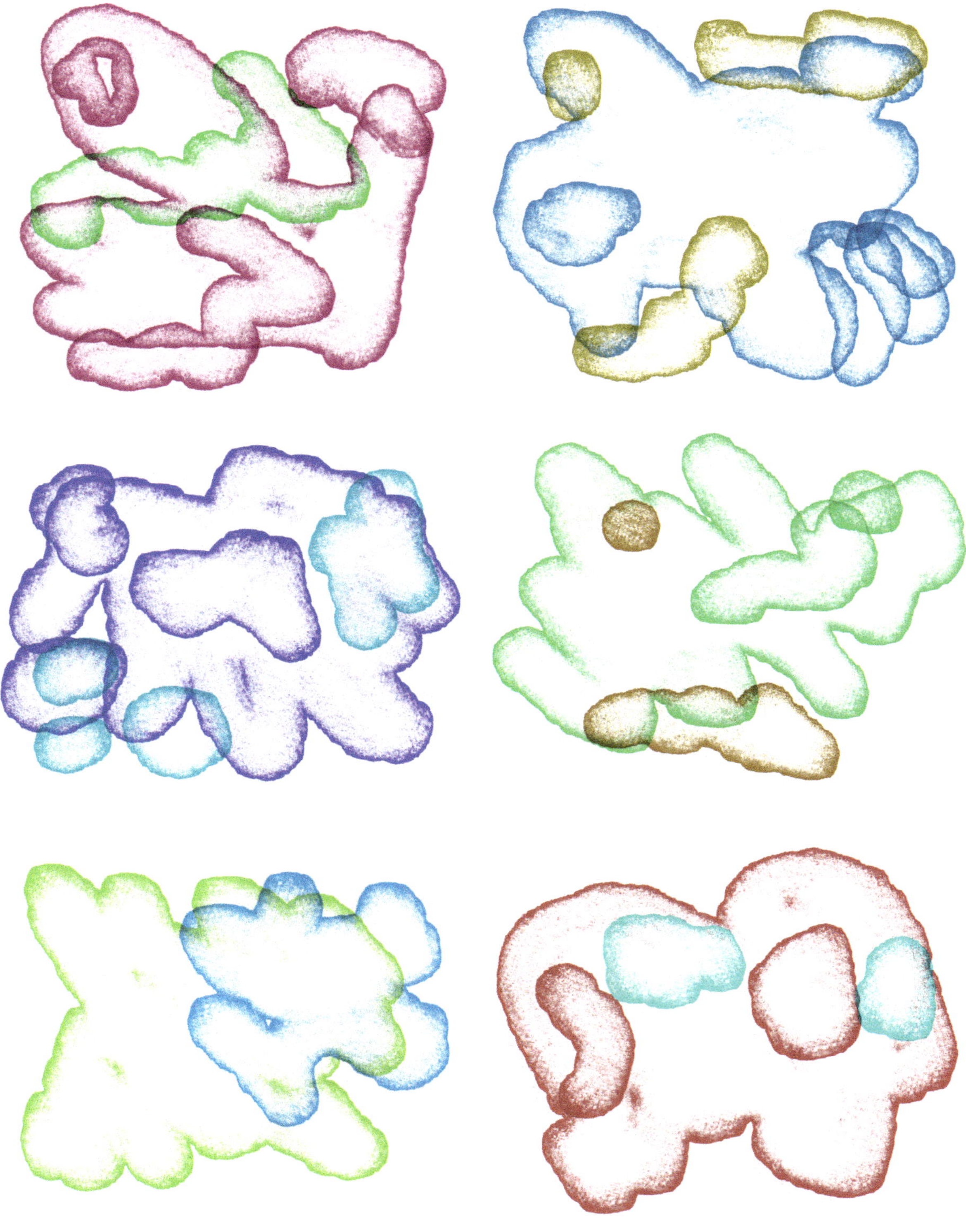

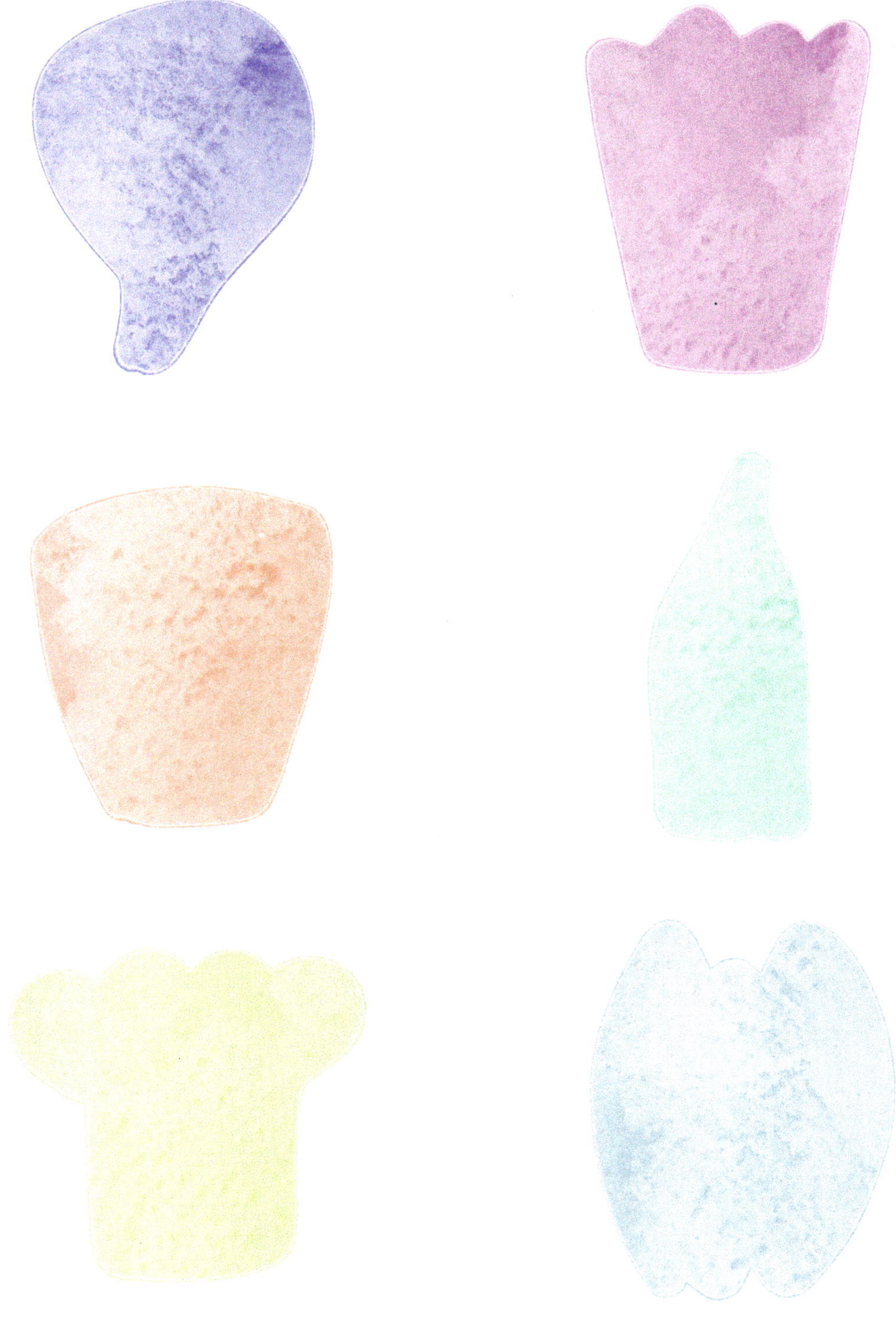

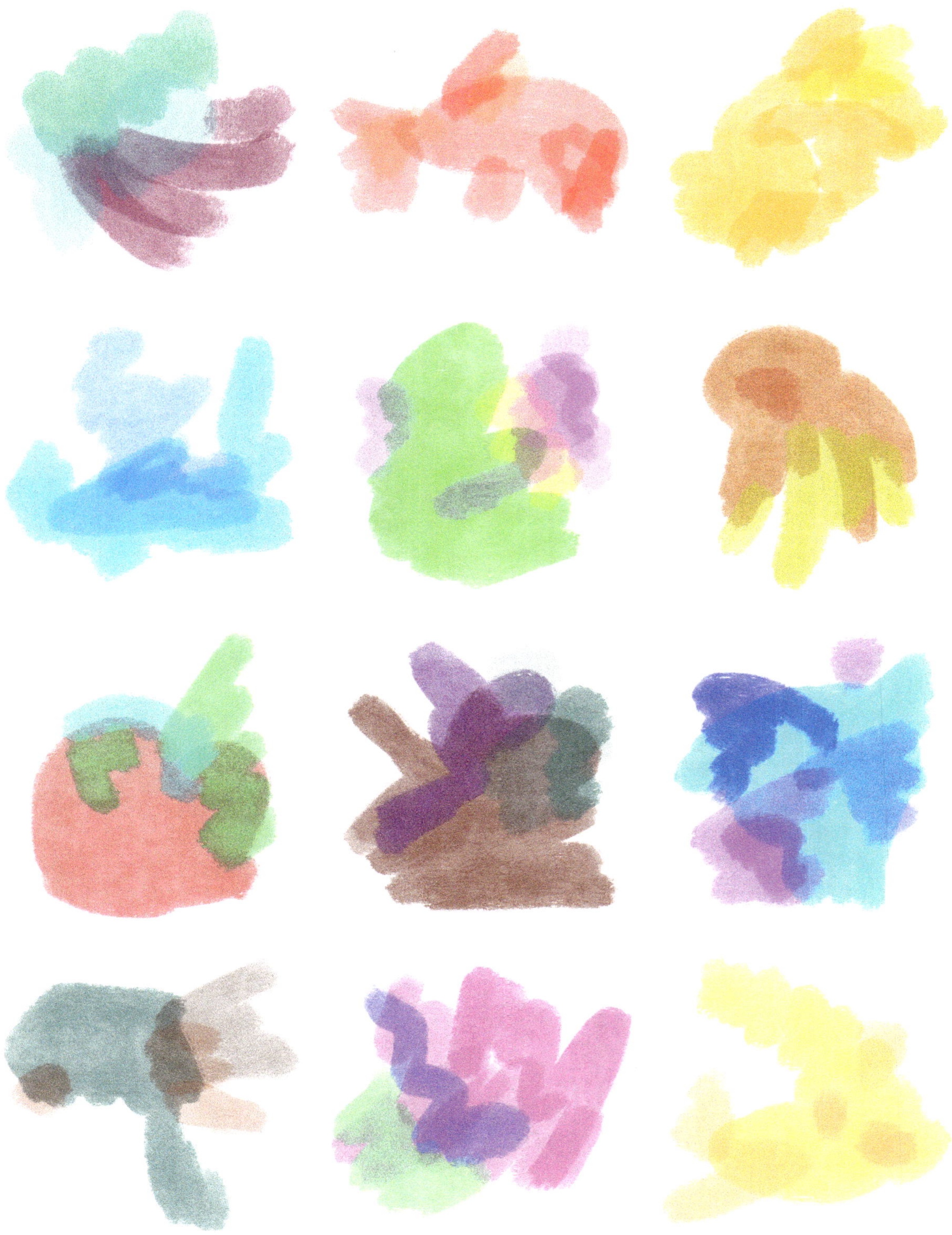

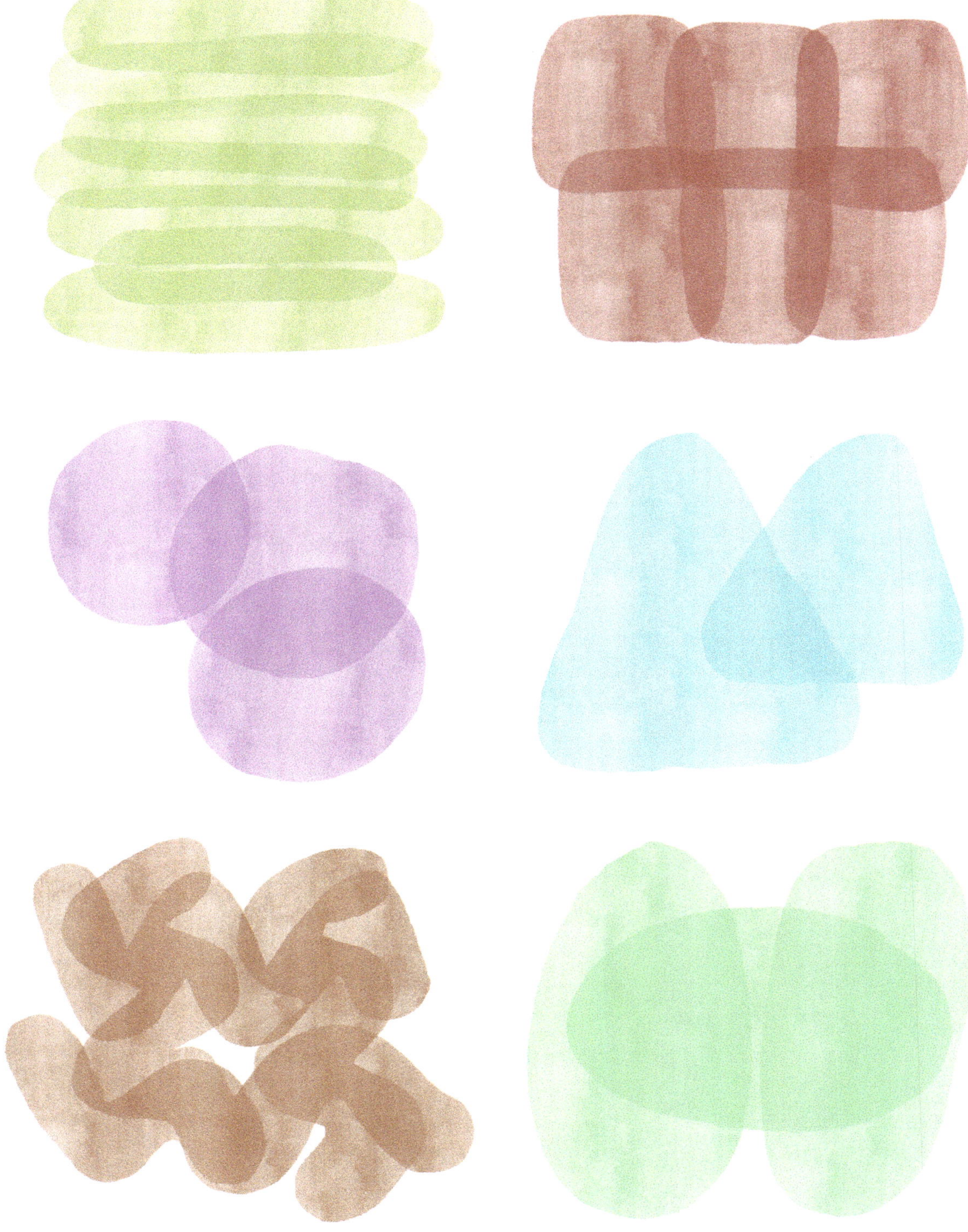

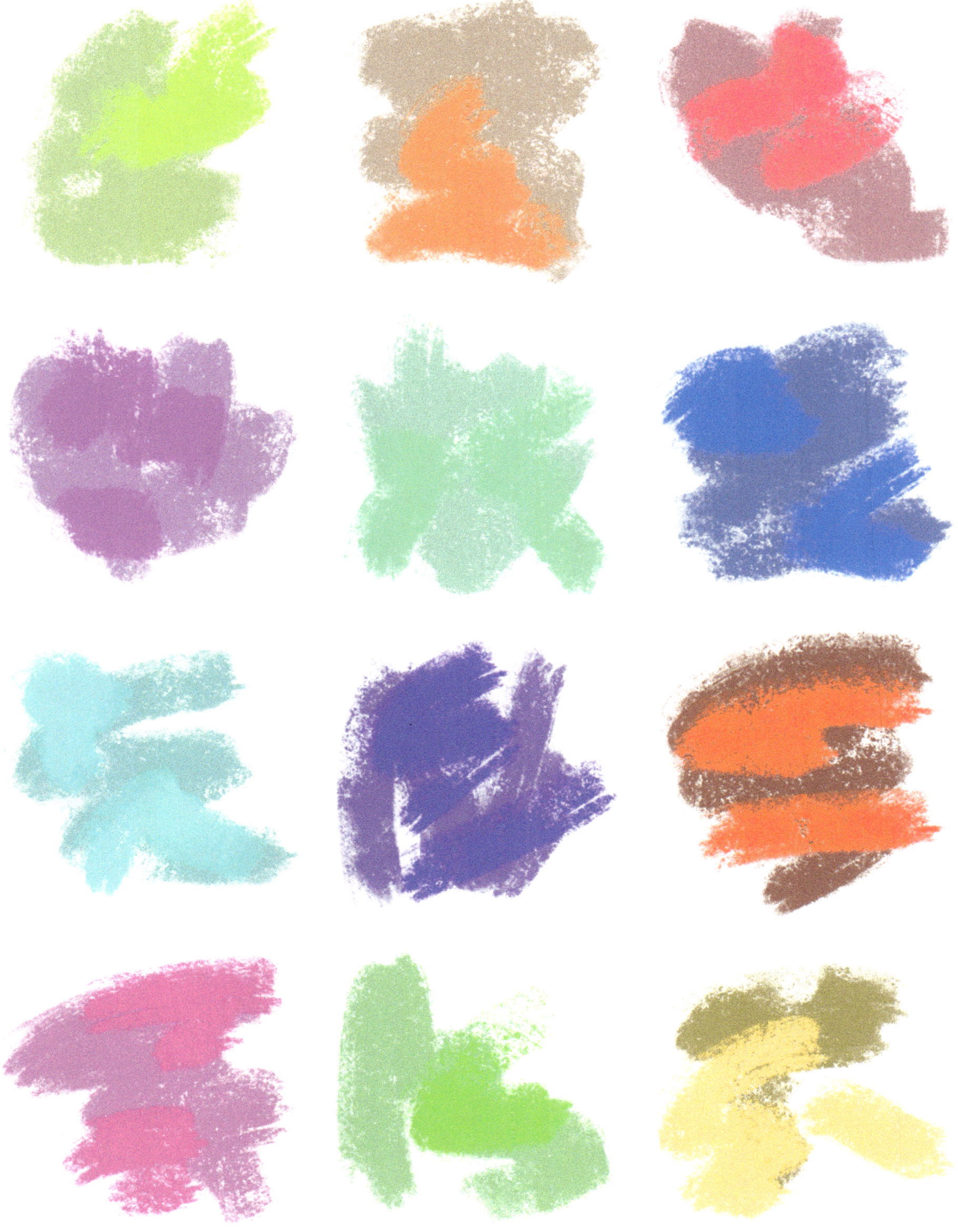

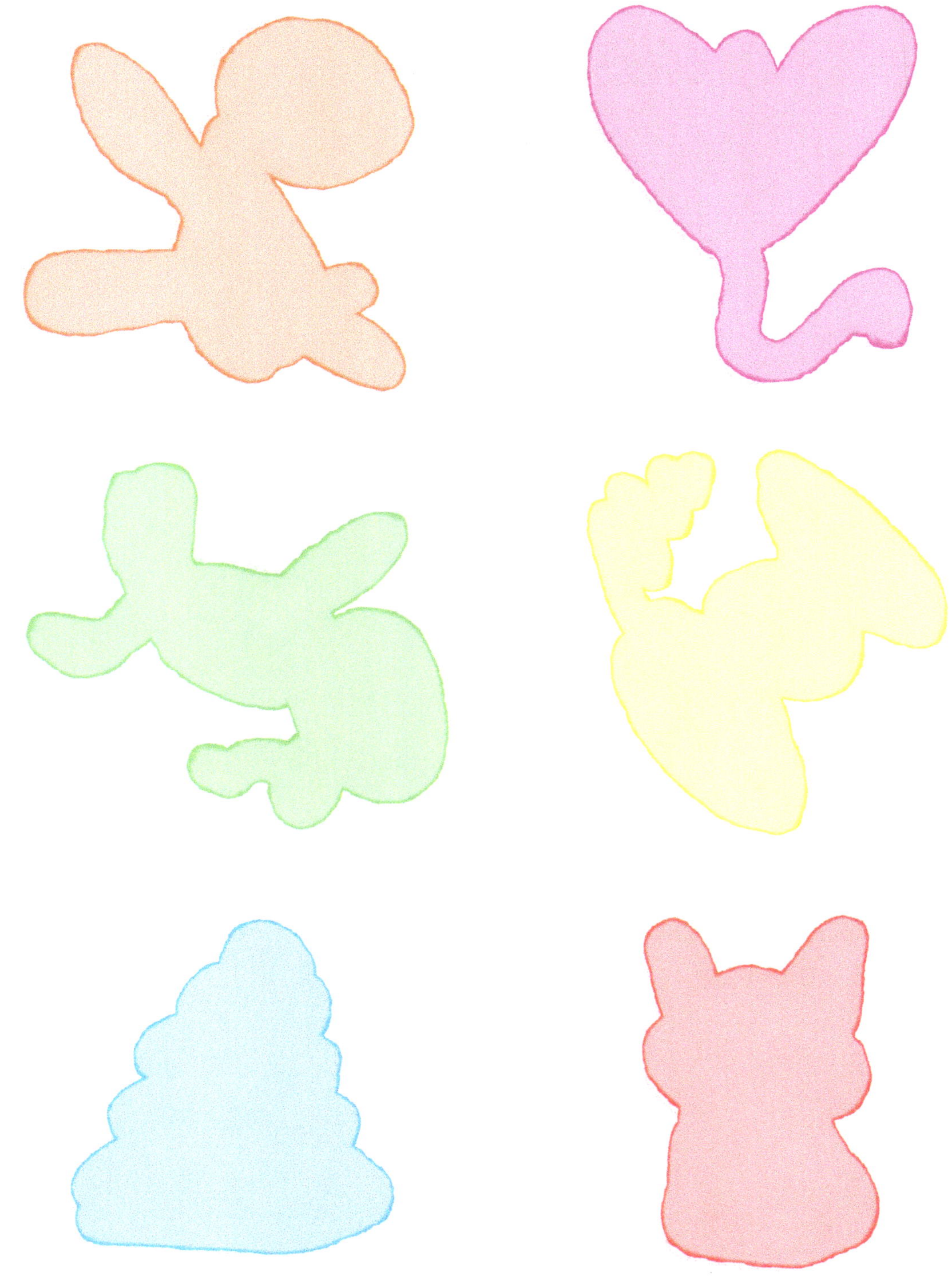

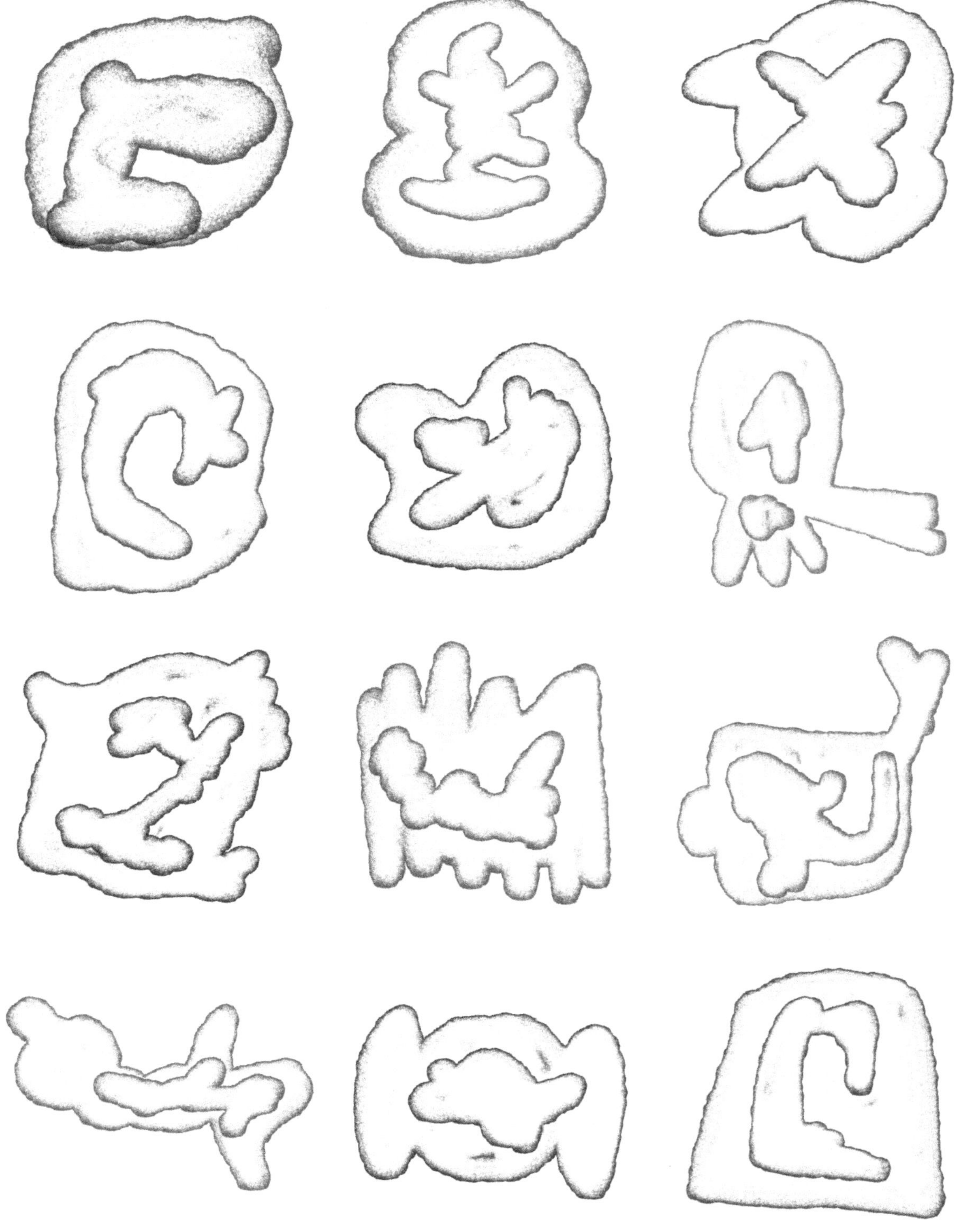

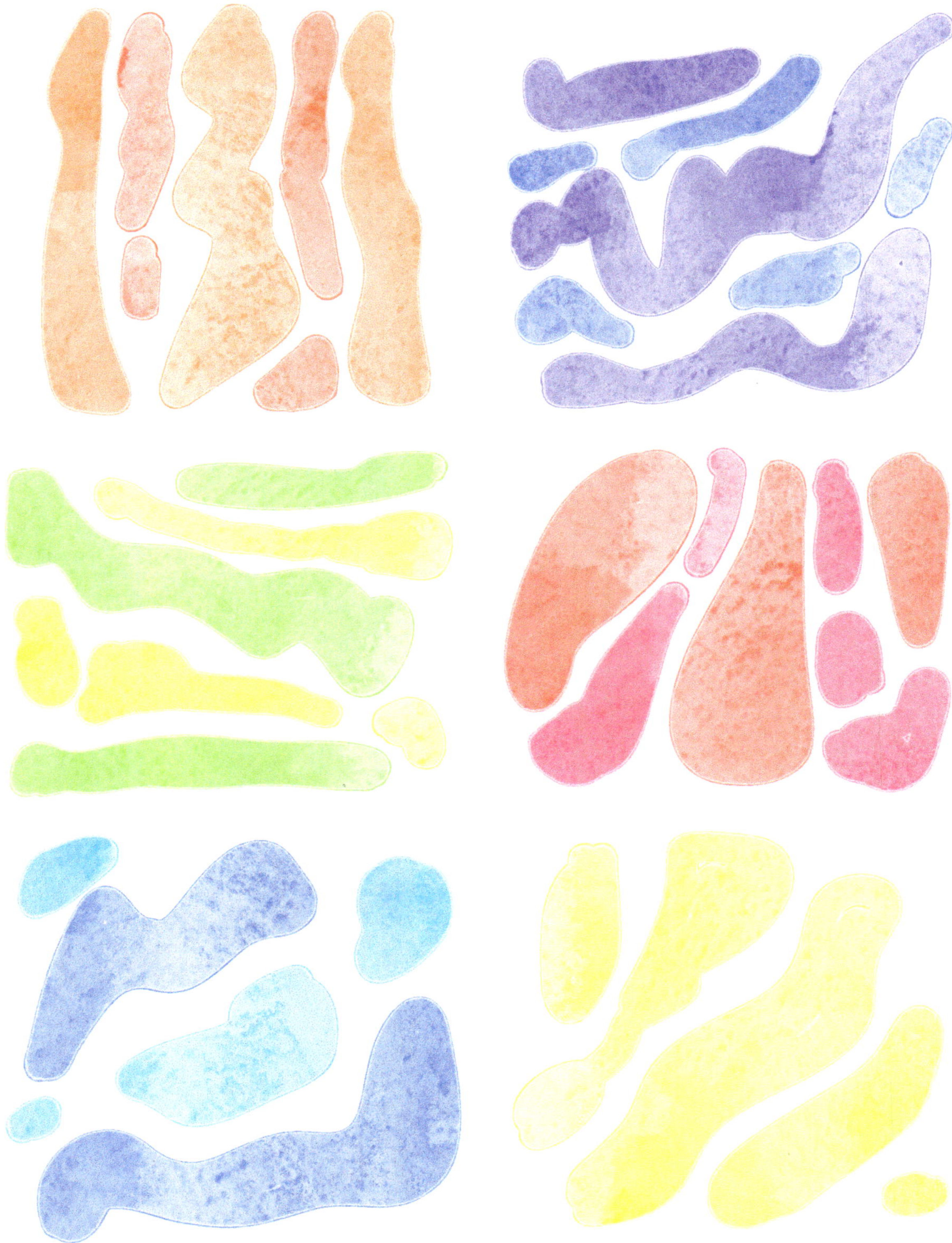

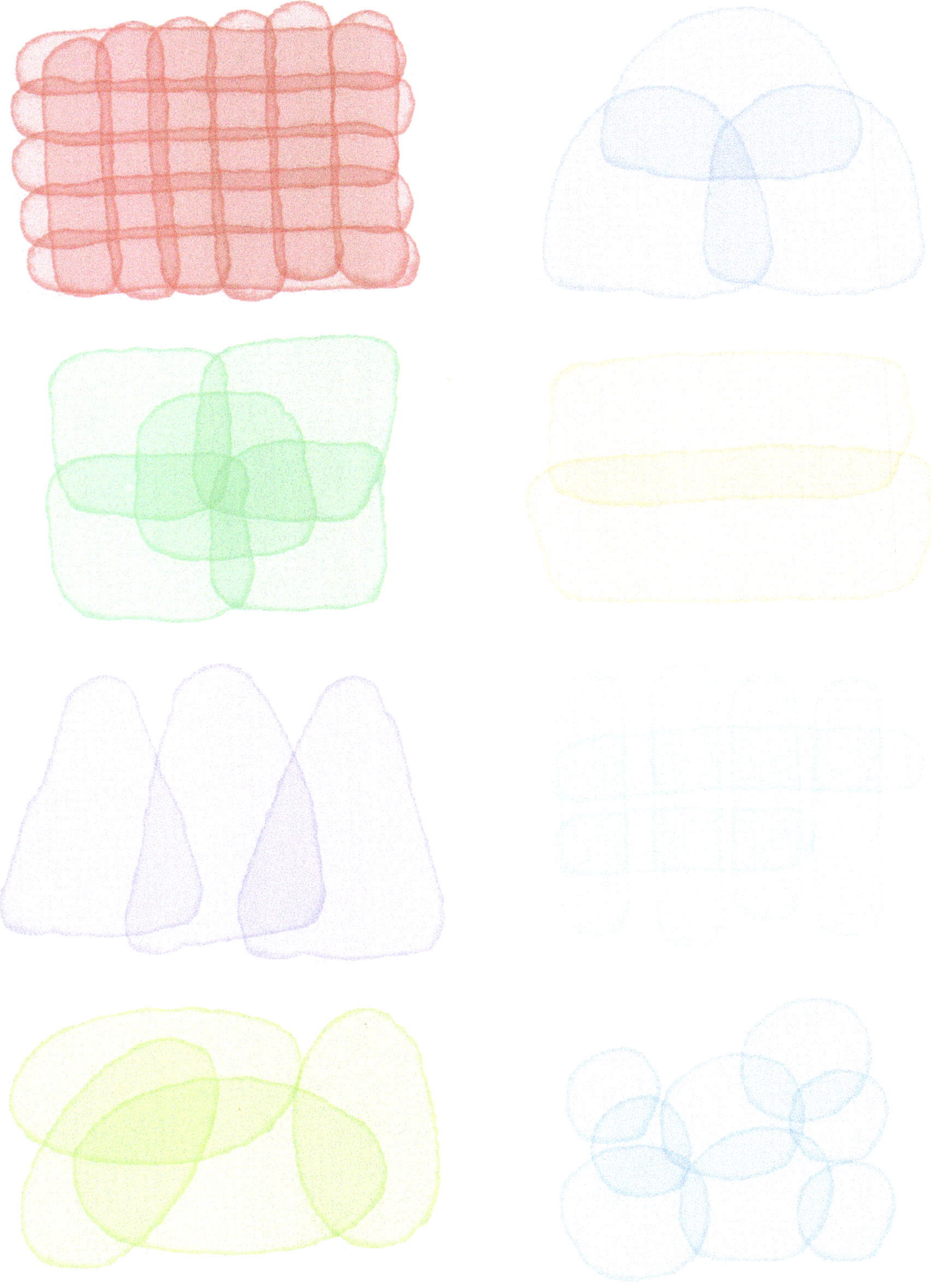

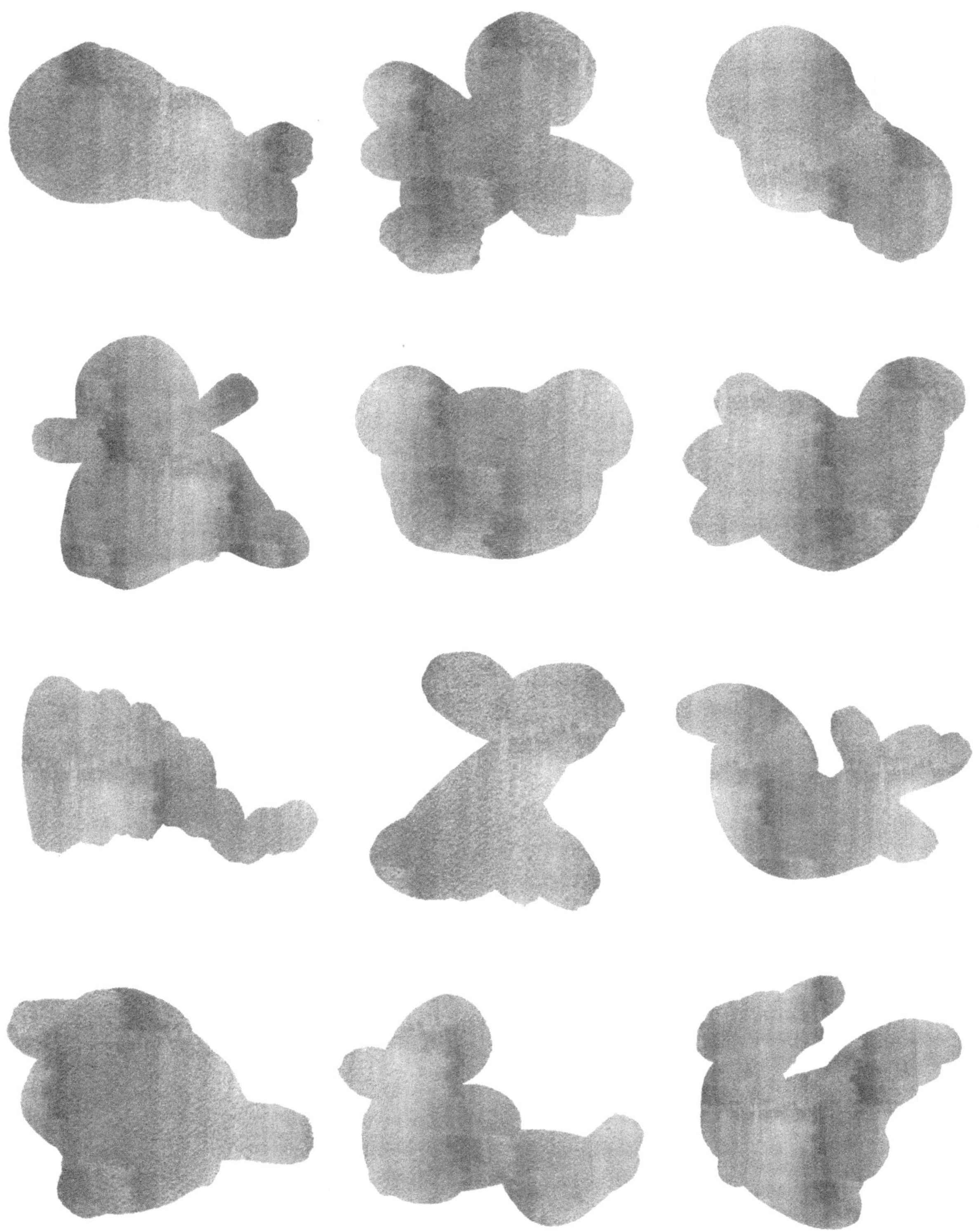

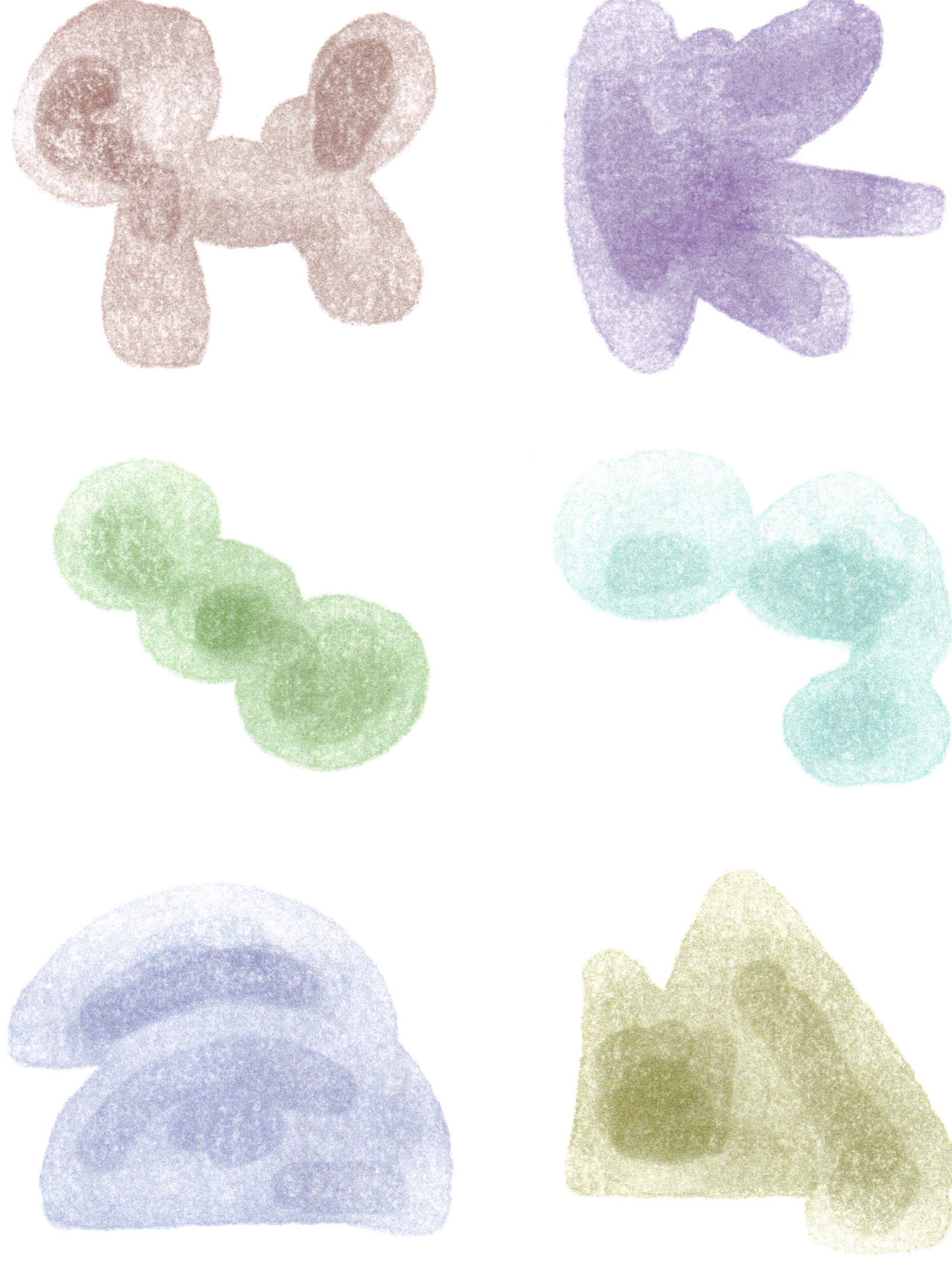

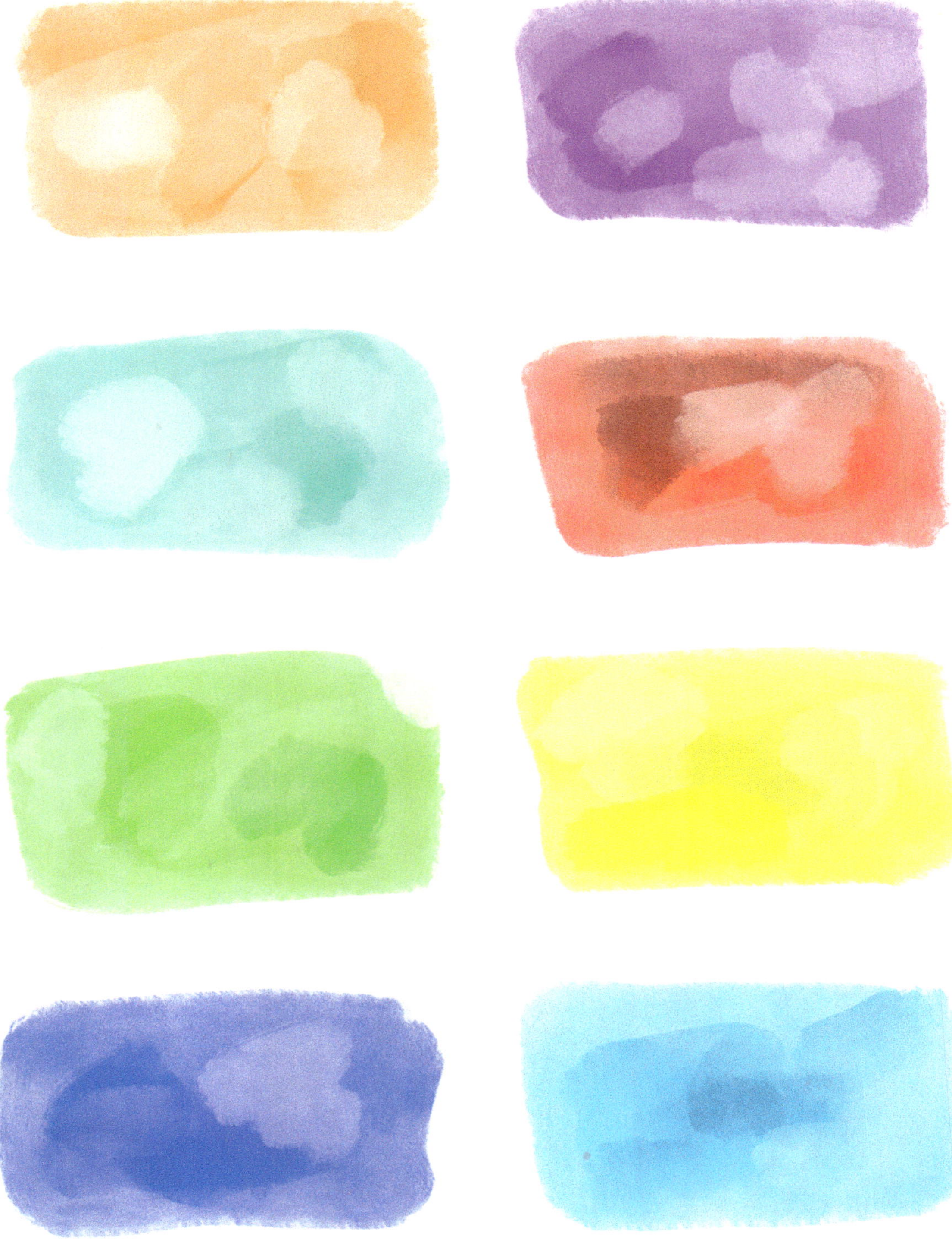

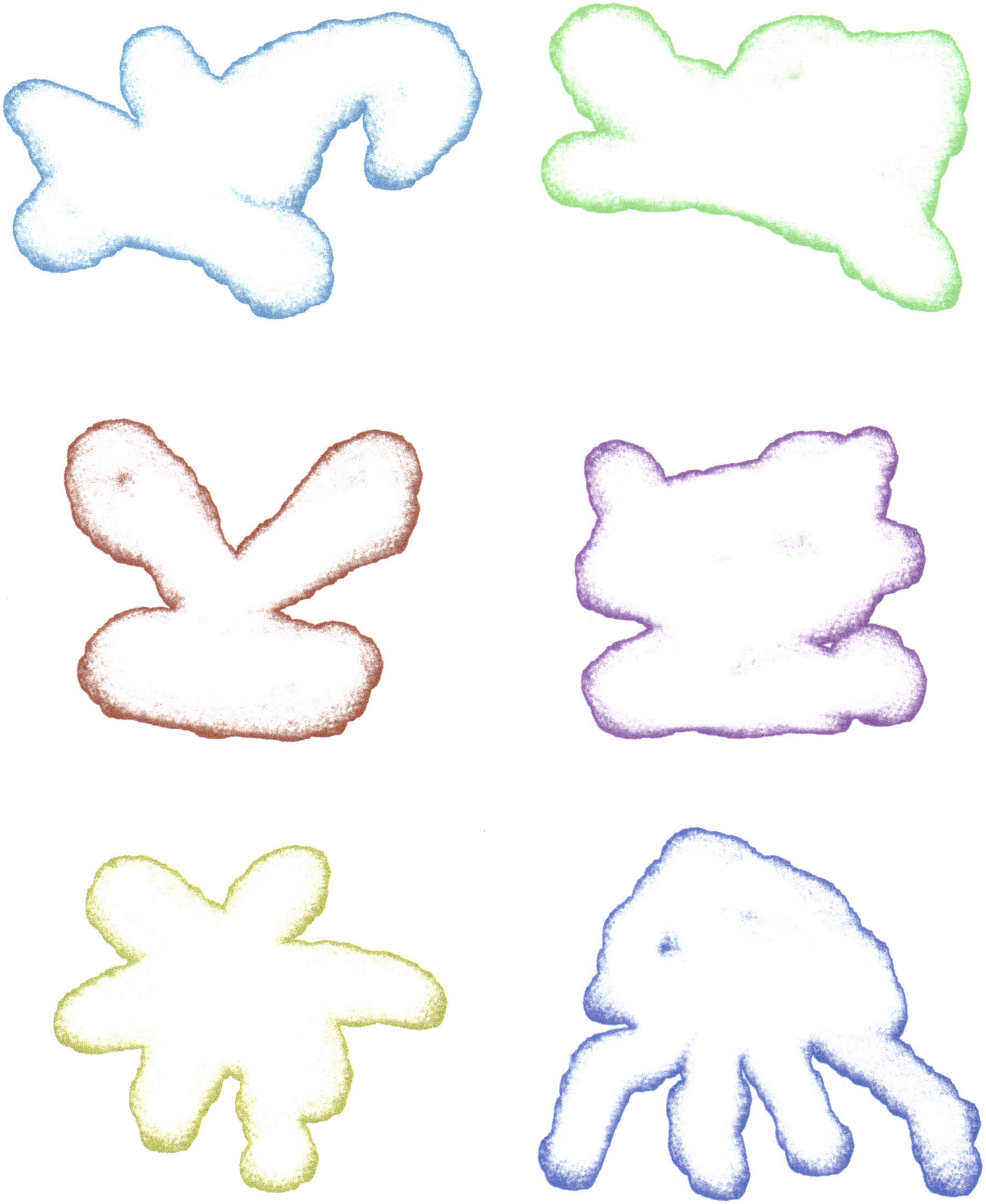

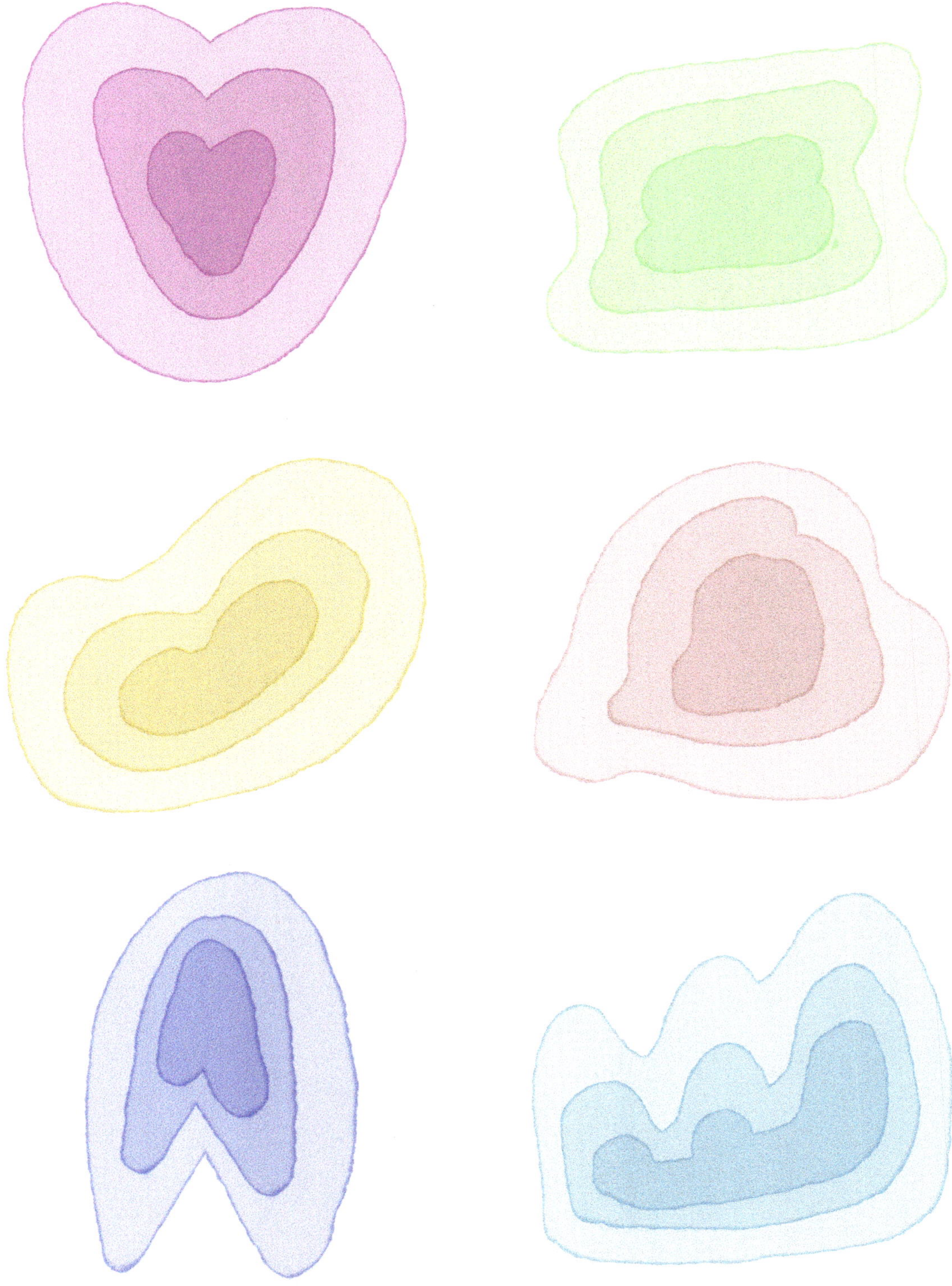

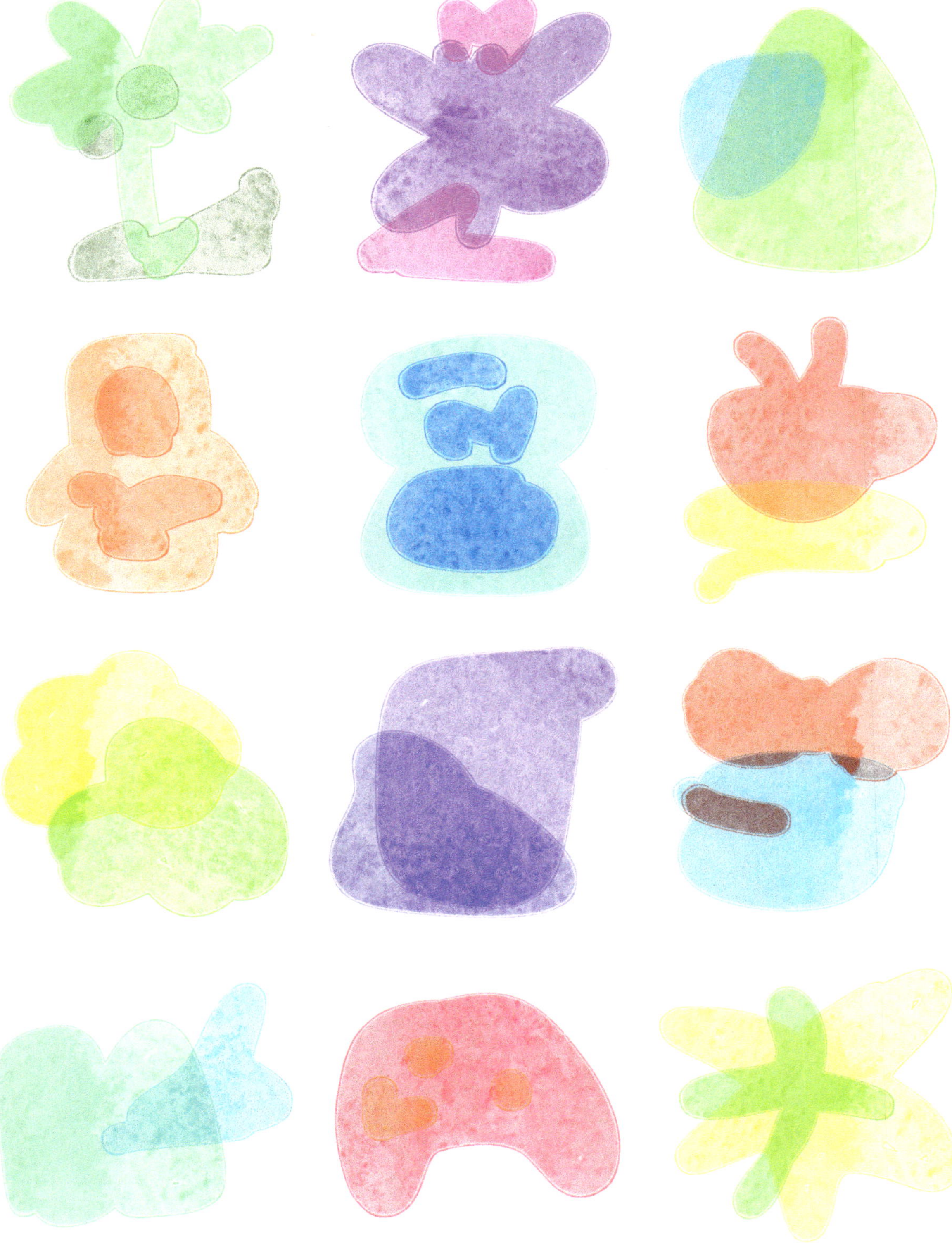

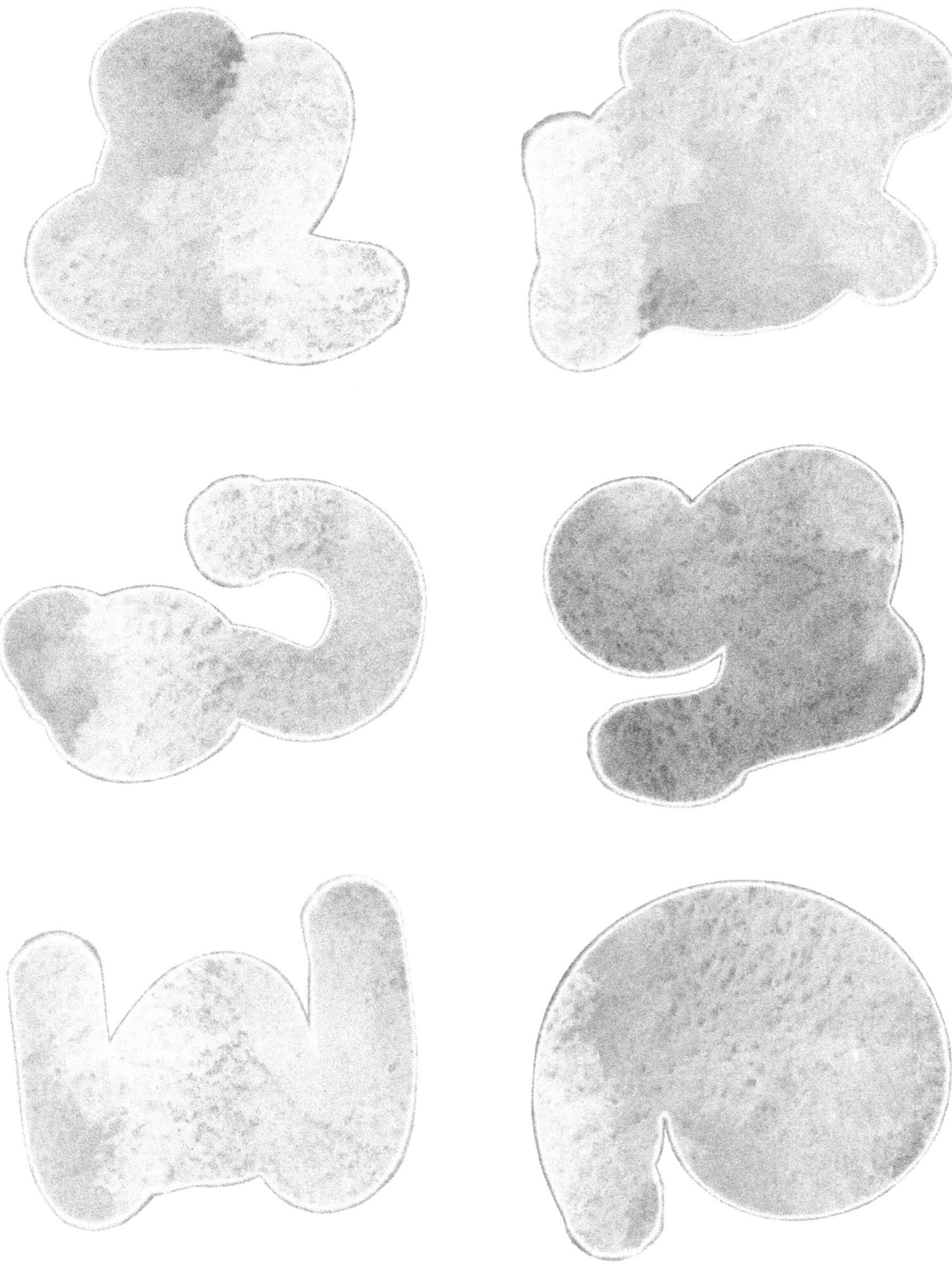

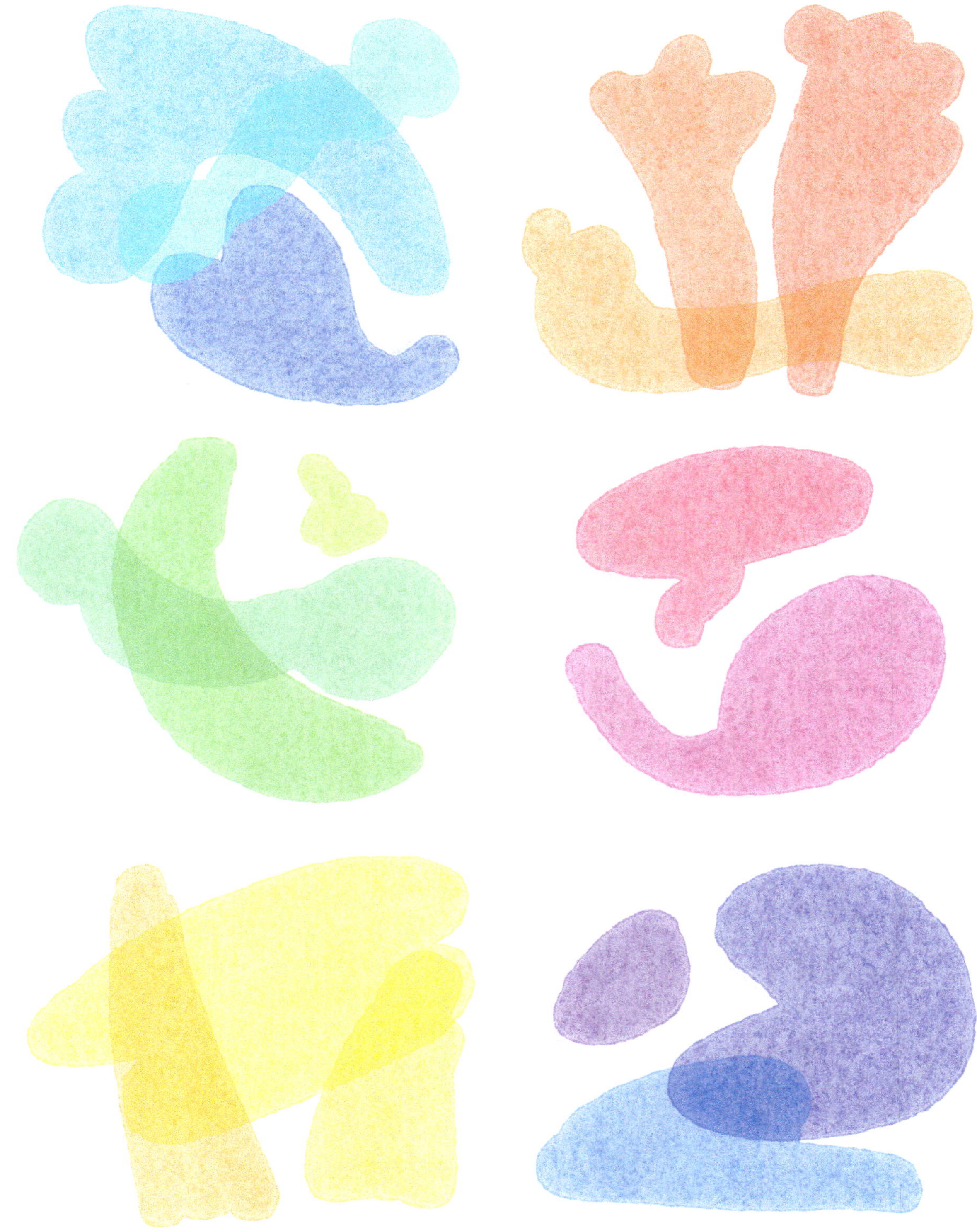

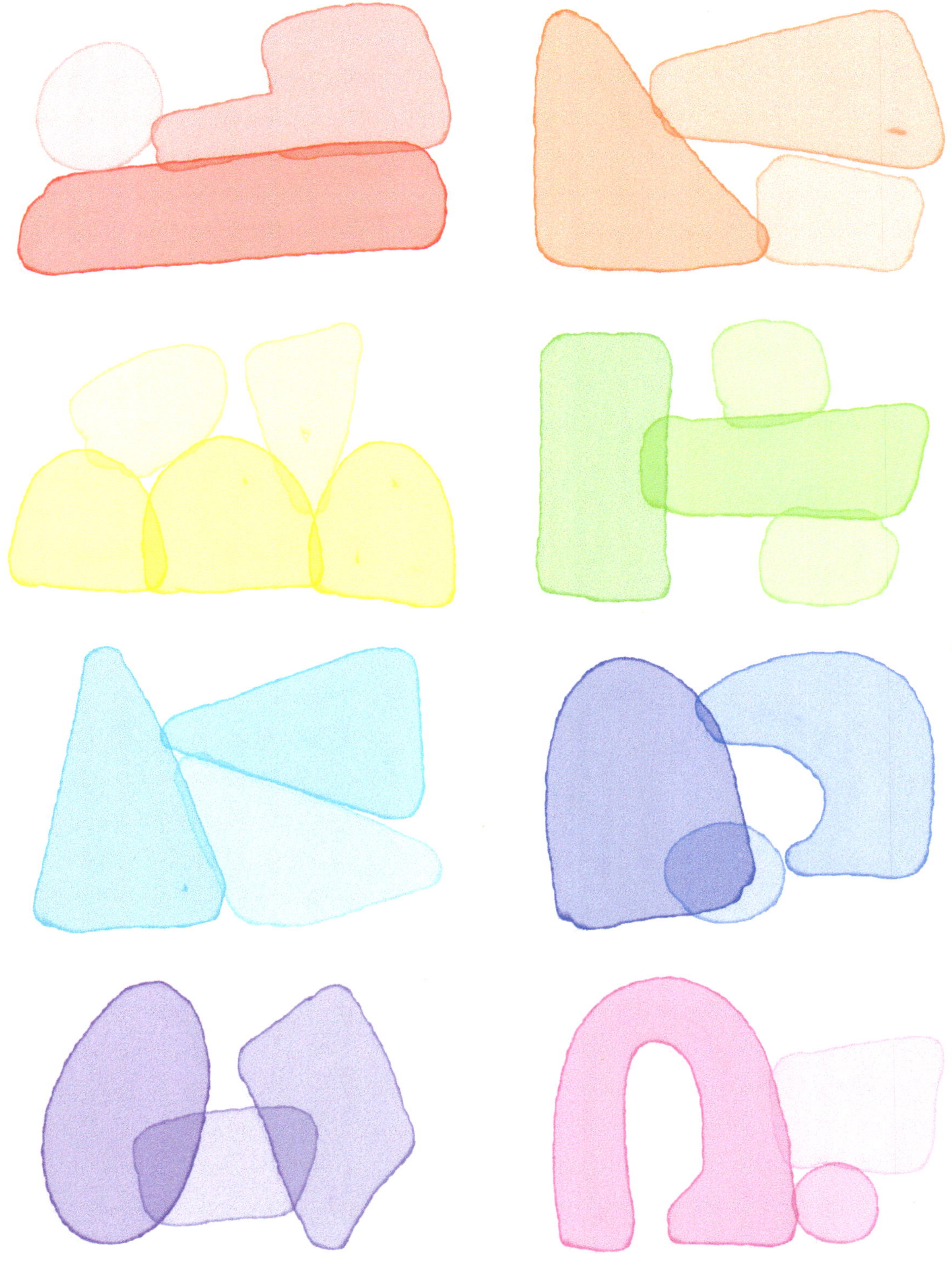

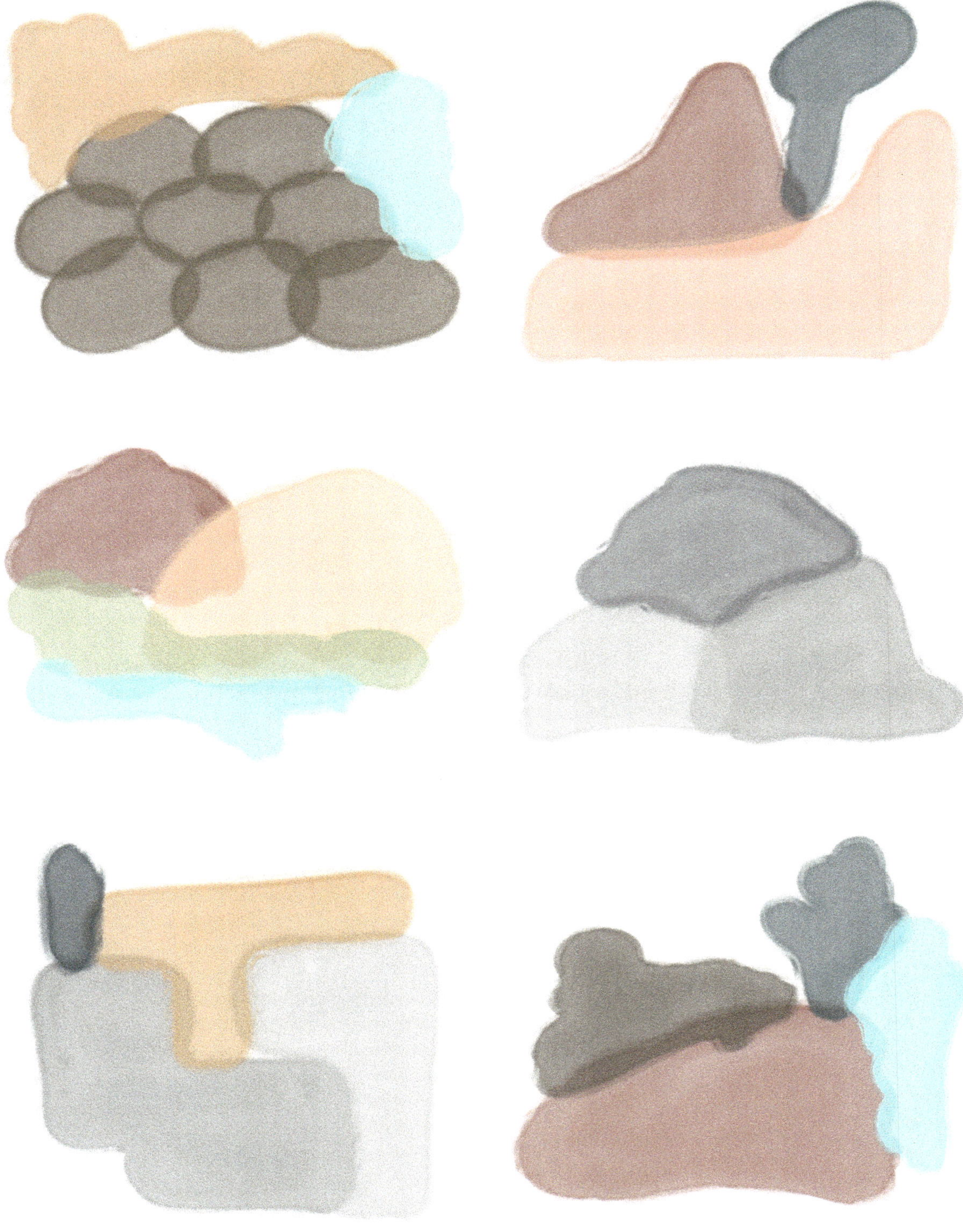

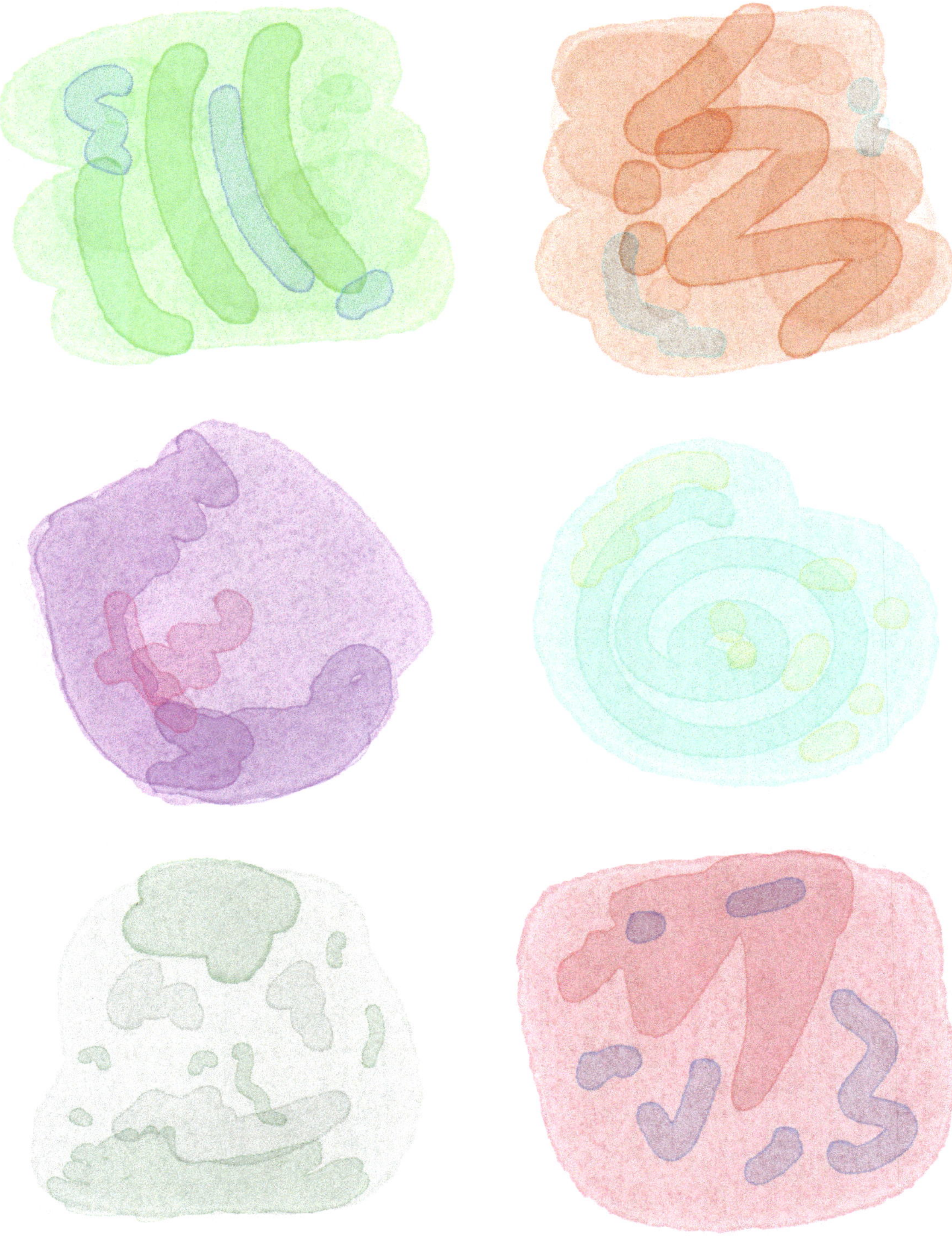

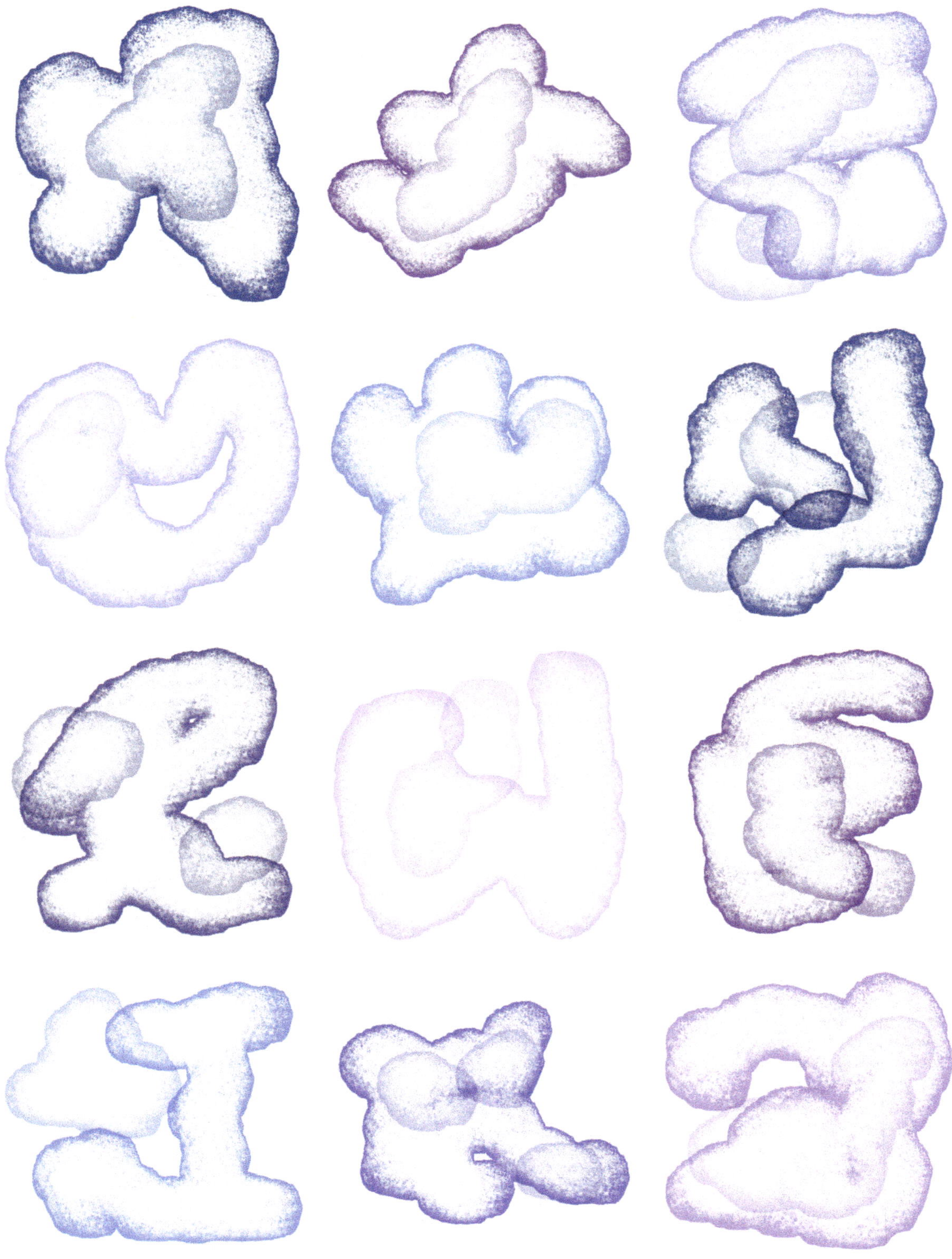

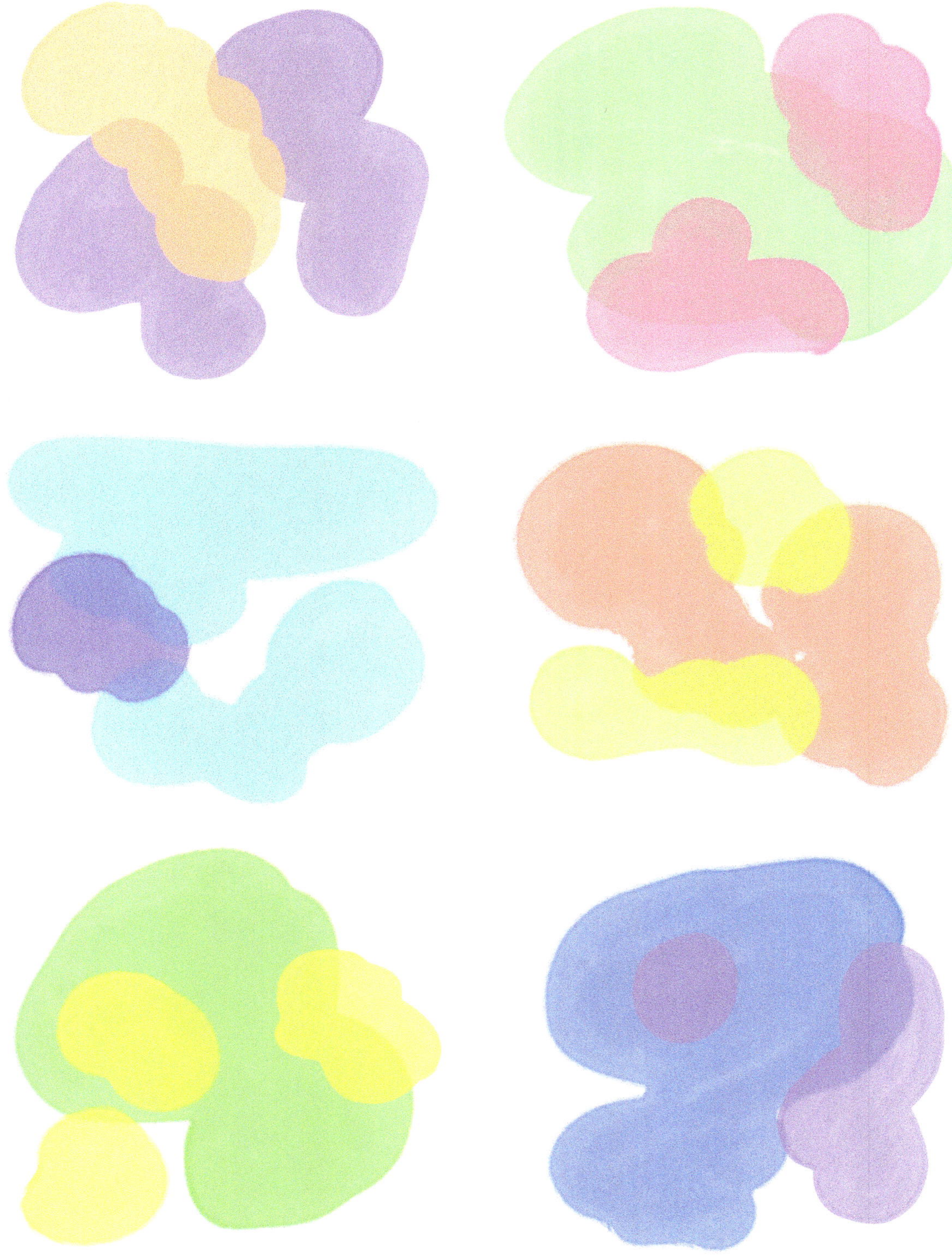

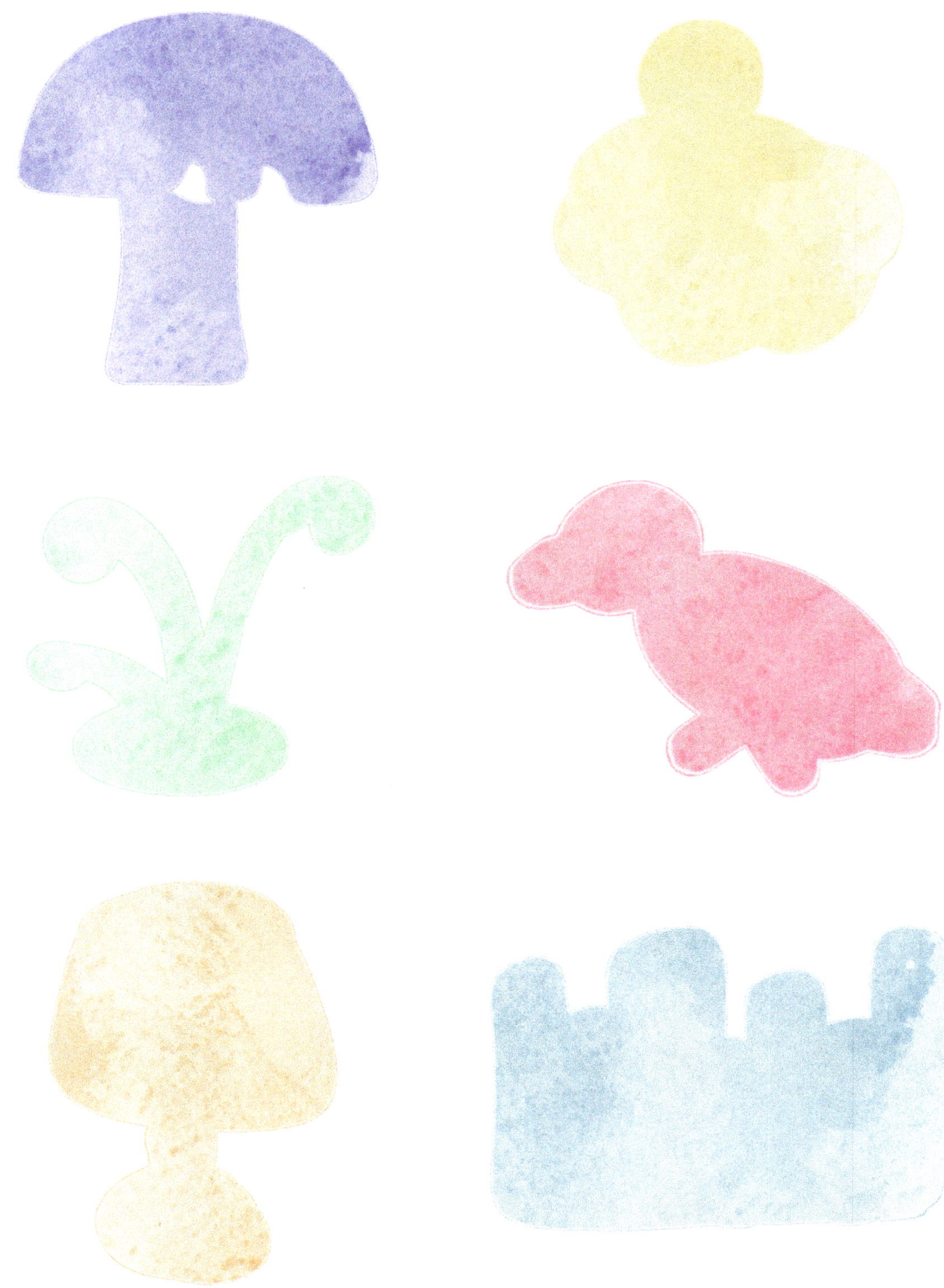

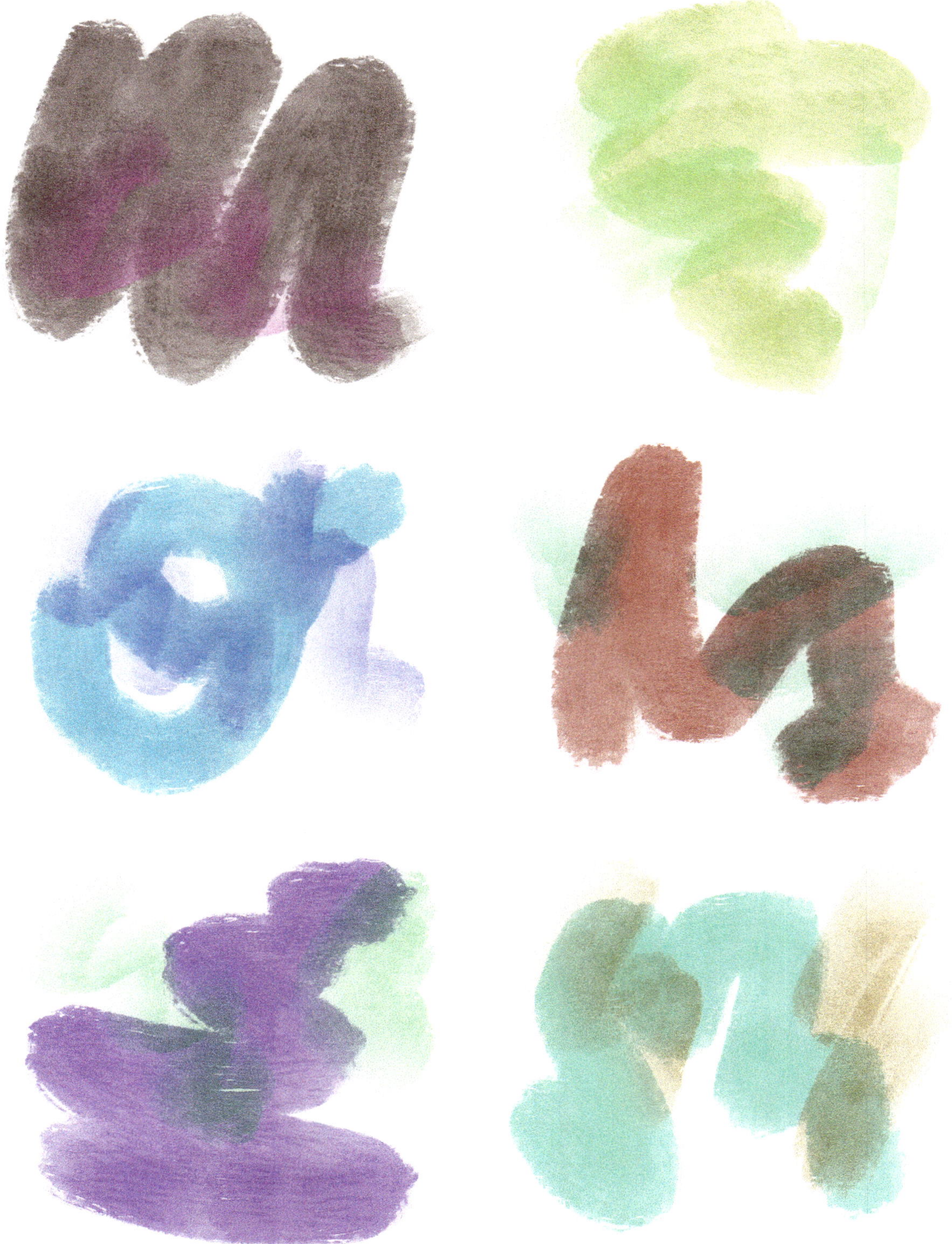

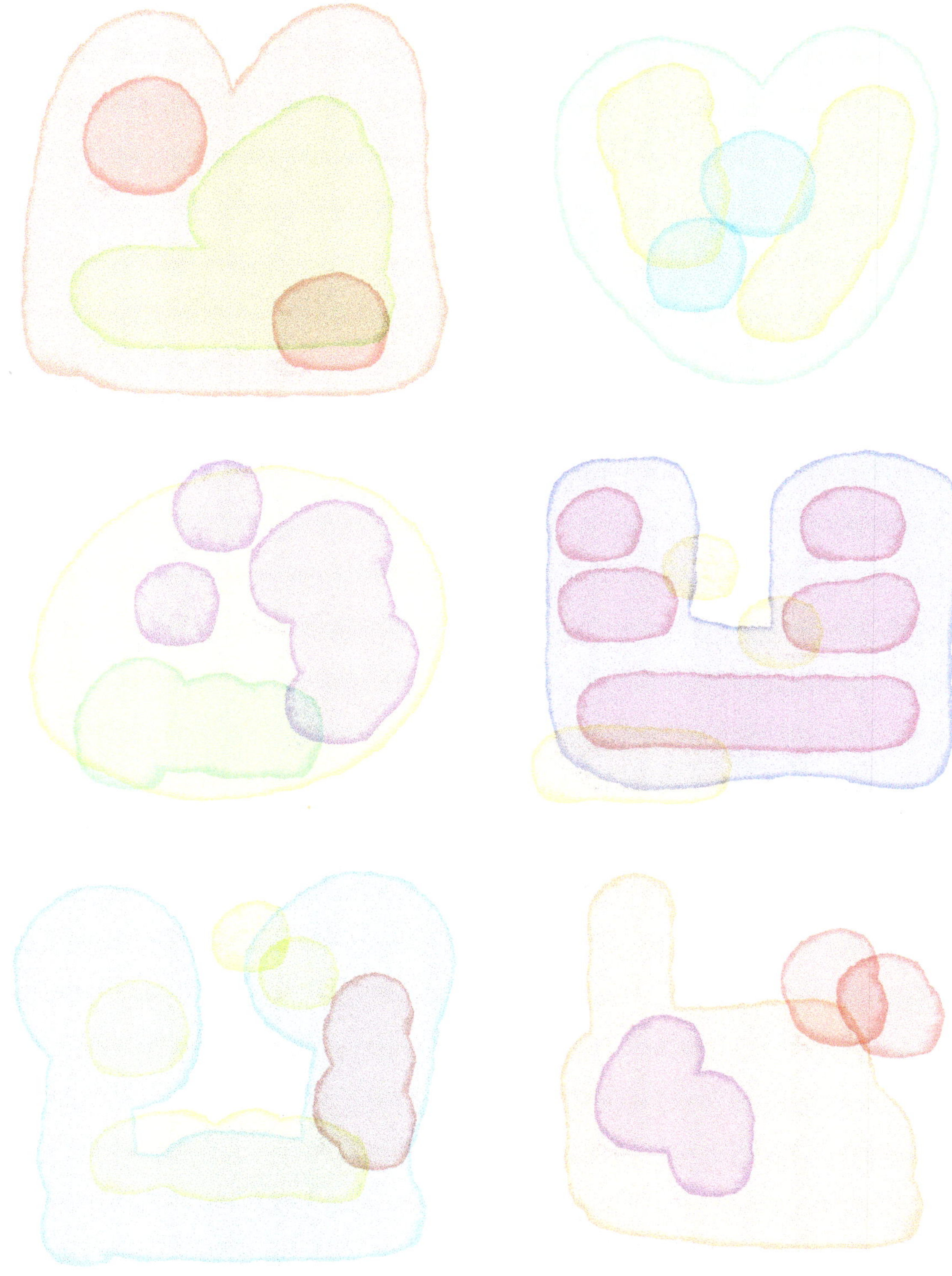

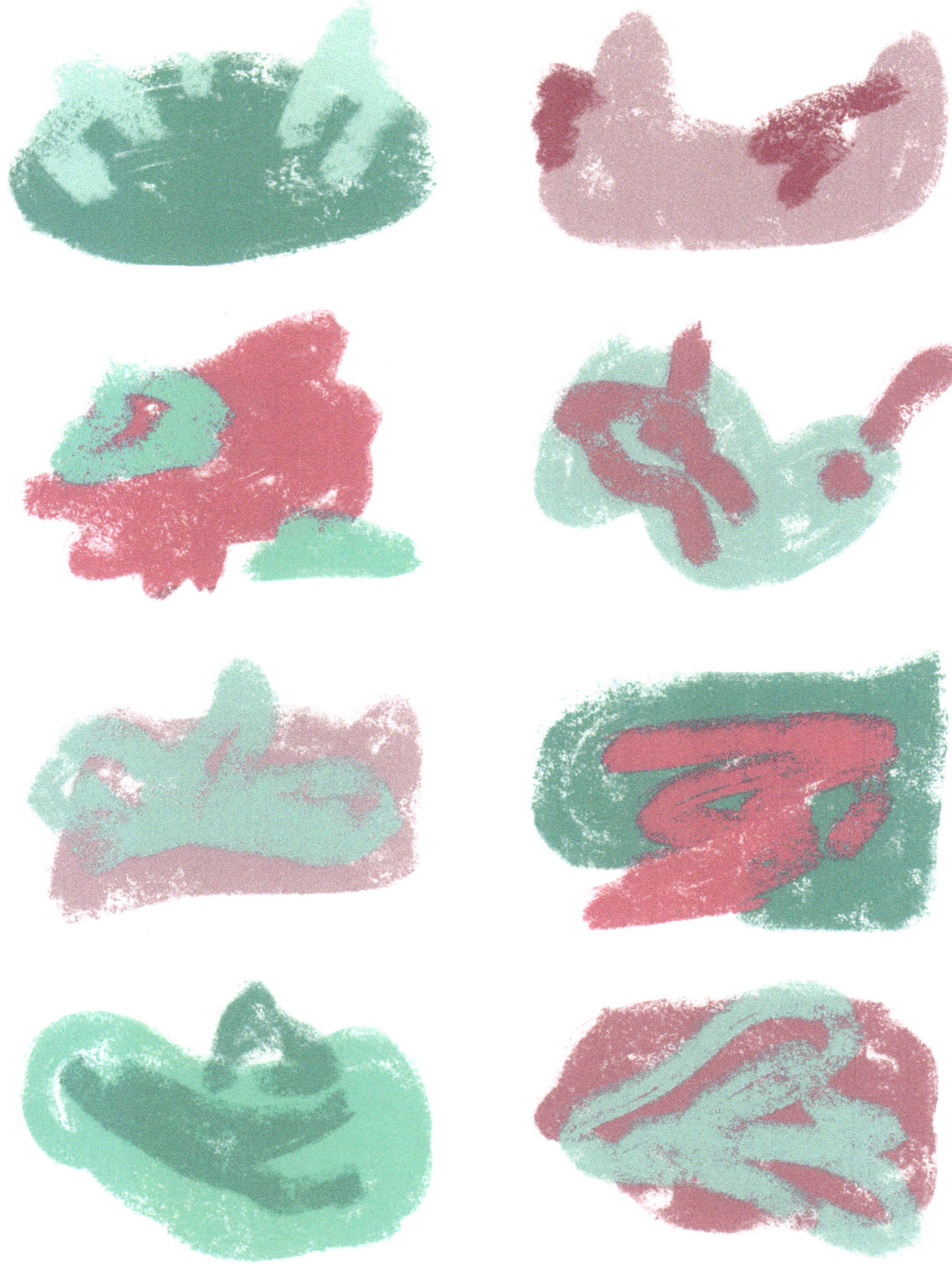

Supply Test Page

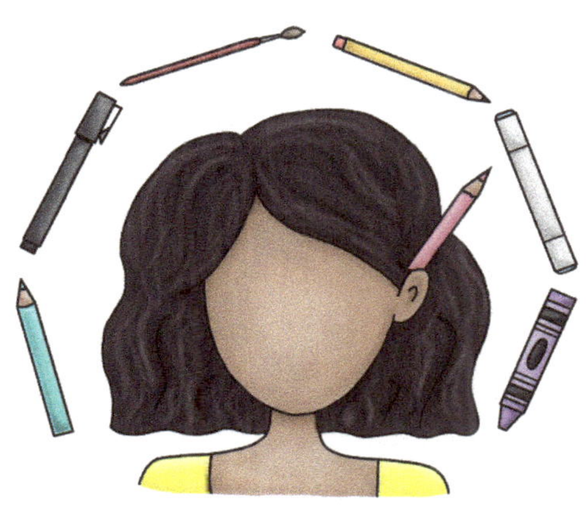

About the Artist

Cassia Dee is a disabled & chronically ill gentle creative. She lives with her husband and their sweet maltipoo Penelope and is passionate about making books a little bit more accessible to the everyday busy person, left-handers, and the chronically ill.

Author: Mindful Bliss Bold & Simple Coloring Book

Right & Left-Handed Versions

Shop & Color Palette Corner:

www.CassiaDee.com